THE SHAME BORNE IN SILENCE:
Spouse Abuse in the Jewish Community

Rabbi Abraham J. Twerski, M.D.

MIRKOV PUBLICATIONS, INC.
Pittsburgh, Pennsylvania

MIRKOV PUBLICATIONS,INC.
P.O. Box 81971
Pittsburgh, Pennsylvania 15217
1-(800)-851-8303

Library of Congress Catalog Card Number 96-076747

10 9 8 7 6 5 4 3 2 1

ISBN 0-9648508-1-8

ACKNOWLEDGMENT

I wish to express my sincere appreciation to a number of people whose assistance in preparation of this book was invaluable, either by providing data or constructive editorial comments. They are (alphabetically): Rabbi Moshe Kletenik, Ms. Phyllis Kuhr, M.A., Ms. Shirley Lebovics, M.S.W., Ms. Rachel Pill, M.S.W., and my daughter, Sarah Twerski, R.N.

I also received much assistance and encouragement from personnel and volunteers at various services for domestic violence problems and Jewish Family and Children's Services. I beg forgiveness if I have omitted people who deserve special mention. My thanks to all of them.

INTRODUCTION

This book has been quite difficult for me to write, perhaps because I had to overcome my resistance to acknowledging that the problem of spouse abuse does indeed exist among Jews. We are no doubt influenced by early life experiences, and I can remember nothing in my home other than a husband-wife relationship of mutual caring and utmost respect. The thought that a husband can raise a hand against his wife was totally alien to me.

I was also subject to the widespread cultural belief that wife abuse simply does not exist among Jews, and that in the non-Jewish population, daughters are told to try to get a Jewish husband because "Jewish husbands do not drink, gamble, or beat their wives." I remember in my childhood study of Torah learning that Hagar was an Egyptian princess who could have married into royalty, but sought instead to become a member of the patriarch Abraham's household because of the serenity and blessing that prevailed therein.

As my psychiatric practice progressed and I began to specialize in the treatment of alcoholism and drug addiction, I was surprised to find that the incidence of such problems among Jews was not negligible, and that cases occurred even among traditionally observant families. I also noticed that because of the stigma associated with these problems, Jewish families were most reluctant to seek help because it meant exposing the problem and possibly being stigmatized. But when I saw the tragedy and ruin that resulted from untreated cases of alcoholism and the harm that was being inflicted on young lives because of failure to treat the problem among parents, I could not keep my silence. I wrote articles in the Anglo-Jewish Press, and traveled from city to city, addressing Jewish lay audiences, rabbinical associations, and counselors of Jewish social agencies. I also became active in the JACS organization (Jewish Alcoholics, Chemically Dependent, and Significant Others). I am pleased that these efforts have borne fruit, and that the problems of chemical dependency and gambling are being more widely recognized and treated, with the salvation of many lives, marriages and families.

I responded to my initial awareness of instances of spouse abuse with the same response that so many people had toward that of alcoholism. "Sure, there was the town *shikker,* but he was the exception. The aphorism '*shikker is a goy,'* is still valid." And so I wished to believe that the one or two cases of spouse abuse that I encountered were "freakish", and were merely anomalous occurrences, rare exceptions to the rule that the sacred institution of Jewish marriage is not subject to abuse.

But alas! Calls kept coming in, and in my contact with professional counselors across the country and in Israel, my naivete was shattered. Perhaps the incidence among Jews was not the astronomical number that exists in the non-Jewish population, but neither is it an isolated phenomenon which can be ignored.

A doctor friend of mine told me that he had five hospital admissions for obvious alcohol abuse, and that each time his colleagues had sought to "protect" him from exposure of his problem because that might have jeopardized his license to practice medicine and earn his livelihood. His untreated alcoholism progressed and resulted in the breakup of his marriage, and it eventually also cost him his hospital privileges. He subsequently wrote an article entitled "The Conspiracy of Silence," in which he states that with all their good intentions and "kindness," his colleagues allowed him to destroy himself.

I began to be haunted by the concept of "Do not stand idly by while your neighbor's blood is being spilled" (*Leviticus* 19:16), which the Talmud interprets to mean that one has an obligation to divert harm from coming to another person. When staffs of social agencies told me that their efforts to alert the Jewish community to the problem of spouse abuse were being ignored, and that I should address the problem because with my credentials as a rabbi and psychiatrist I might be better believed, I began to feel uneasy at remaining silent. Someone then pointed out to me that the Talmud says that "Anyone who has the ability to correct a situation and is derelict in doing so, bears the responsibility for whatever results therefrom" (*Shabbos* 54b), I realized that I have no option, and that I must speak out.

There will be those who will say that such subjects should not be aired publicly, and that to do so is a *chilul Hashem*, a disgrace to the sanctity of Judaism, to even imply that Jewish husbands can be wife batterers. I understand that position, but if I must choose between being reprimanded by those who believe that this problem should be concealed or by a wife who has suffered (along with her children) from an abusive husband, and could not receive help because no one believed her, I know where I must make my choice.

Battered wives have often turned to their parents or to their spiritual leaders for help. Very often they have been told to avoid disrupting the family unit, to preserve *shalom bayis* (peace in the home), and that things will work out. Parents and rabbis are good and considerate people. They mean well, but they may have no way of knowing that their advice is wrong and could be deadly.

In our daily confession *(oshamnu)*, we list a number of sins to which a human being may succumb because of anger, greed, lust, and various temptations that may override a person's better judgment. We also confess to *yoatznu ra*, "we have given bad advice." Why on earth would anyone do that? What gain or pleasure could possibly result from misleading someone else? Surely we are not suspect of being sadistic and deriving pleasure from malicious behavior.

No, we are not in any way suspect of being perverse. *Yoatznu ra,* means that we have mistakenly and unintentionally given bad advice, which we thought to be good advice and beneficial to those who sought our counsel. It is much like someone telling a friend, "Try this medication. It did wonders for me," without knowing that the other person has a condition for which this medication may be very harmful.

Unless we understand the problems of spouse abuse, we may unwittingly give bad advice to our children, our friends, our clients, and our parishioners. This book is intended to provide insights into the problem from actual cases, as well as several observations on Torah values and an overview of what the conditions are in society that must be considered when dealing with spouse abuse.

Spouse abuse can be subdivided into (1) physical abuse or battering, (2) emotional or verbal abuse, and (3) sexual abuse. Battering cases are predominantly husbands aggressing against wives, with the ratio of about 16:1. There are no valid statistics on emotional abuse, but there are incidents of the husband being the victim of this type of abuse. Both types are important, and damaging to all family members. However, battering must be given special attention because this can be a real threat to life and limb. Since battering demands immediate attention, there will be greater focus on the wife as victim of abuse in this book. This by no means diminishes the need to recognize and properly manage emotional abuse where the husband is the recipient. Also, there is a need to recognize *that emotional abuse is indeed abuse.* Too often it is disregarded by some rabbis who may dismiss the woman's complaint, because "Women are overly sensitive."

It is not my intent to disrupt marriages. To the contrary, ignoring and denying spouse abuse is what will ultimately result not only in dissolution of marriages, but also in an impact on the children that will cause them to be dysfunctional spouses and parents when they mature and marry. Emotional abuse may precede physical violence, and early intervention at this point may forestall battering. If spouse abuse is identified and properly managed early, there is hope for the survival of the marriage. However, the survival of the marriage is contingent on the abuser's choosing to make changes in himself. Allowing abuse to continue by making believe it does not exist is certain to undermine the relationship and eventually lead to its demise.

Let us begin to look at this very painful problem with as much open mindedness and objectivity as we can muster. Needless to say, all names cited are fictitious, and in those instances where accurate description of all details might have resulted in violating anonymities, non-essential details have been omitted.

Chapter 1

RESIGNATION

Bella twisted her handkerchief and bit her lips, fighting back tears. "I never thought it would come to this," she said.

"Our youngest son, Marvin, was Bar Mitzvah three weeks ago. It was beautiful. Marvin led the services in the synagogue like a pro. The Bar Mitzvah party went off without a hitch. Both my parents and Bernie's parents were glowing with *nachas*. As happy as I was, my heart was breaking, because I had decided that I wouldn't ruin things for Marvin. There was no reason he should suffer, but that once his Bar Mitzvah was over, I was going to leave the marriage."

"When did you make that decision?" I asked.

"Just about two years ago. Bernie and I had had a spat. It wasn't much different than the ones we had before. I told him that it was ridiculous that I could not sign checks and that I wanted to have my name on our account. He said that two people writing checks on the same account causes too much confusion, and we'd never know how much we had in the bank. I said that I could open up another account in my name, and he said we didn't have enough money for two accounts. We'd been through that before. And then I said that my friend, Helen, thought that was silly, and that another checking account would not cost us anything. Bernie came at me in a rage, 'You're talking about me to your friends,' he screamed. [At this point, the husband felt that his power and control were being threatened by his wife's receiving advice from her friends, hence his anger escalated to physical violence]. He grabbed my arm and twisted it, and I saw a degree of anger in his eyes that I had never seen before.

"Let go of my arm!" I shouted. "You're hurting me." He slapped me across the face and pushed me against the wall. "Don't you ever talk about me to your friends, you bitch," he said. I ran up and locked myself in the bathroom and cried.

"I opened the medicine cabinet and there was a bottle of pain pills that Bernie used for his back, and I thought that if I swallowed the whole bottle I could be at peace, forever. But then what about the kids? It's not their fault, and I have been a good mother to them.

"Bernie didn't speak to me again that night, and the following morning he was as calm as if nothing had happened. [This reaction is in itself a form of abuse, in that the husband's attitude of serenity in contrast to the wife's agitation makes her feel that she must be going crazy.] I thought about it all day, and decided that I was not going to ruin Marvin's Bar Mitzvah. He is a lovely boy and is working very hard for it, but after the Bar Mitzvah I was going to leave him."

"How long had you been married when this incident happened?" I asked.

"Let's see. We're married 19 years, and this was two years ago, which would have been 17 years."

"Had there been a marked change about that time in your husband's behavior?"

"Not really. It was just that it was the first time that he ever got physically rough with me, but his attitude toward me was never much different."

"Never much different since when?"

"Since we were married. Bernie was always a strong-willed person. Things had to be his way because he knew best. My opinion never counted for anything. I found that out soon after we were married, but that didn't appear to be a problem. He loved me, and it seemed we would have a good future. I was happy then."

"When did you discover you were not happy?"

"The first time it really bothered me, it sounds silly, I know, was when I went to buy my parents an anniversary gift. Nothing big. Bernie had given me money which I had put in my coat pocket. As I was leaving the house it began to rain, and I went back in and changed into my raincoat, but I forgot to take the money out of my other coat. When I was going to pay for my purchase at the store, I didn't have the money, and I was so embarrassed. I didn't have a check because, you know, Bernie didn't agree to that."

"Why didn't you just charge it?"

"Charge it? Bernie says charge accounts are what causes families to go bankrupt. I don't have any charge accounts or credit cards."

"That night," she continued, "I told Bernie how stupid I felt at the store and that I had to leave the gift behind because I couldn't pay for it, and he said it was my fault for not taking the money along. I told him I didn't see why I couldn't write a check or have a charge account like my friends do, and he became livid with rage. 'You are not married to your friends' husbands,' he screamed. 'You're married to Bernard A. Segal, and don't you forget that.' But he never touched me then."

"What did you do then?" I asked.

"What was there I could do?" Bella replied. "I just went along. It was only a single incident, and it really was stupid of me to forget to take along the money." [The wife tends to believe what the husband tells her.]

"Did you feel at that time that your husband was too domineering and too controlling?" I asked.

"Not really. He was a good provider, and we had lovely children. I was making a good home for them." [The wife assumes that her sole mission in life is to make a good home, regardless of the degree of personal sacrifice.]

"Didn't you feel sort of disenfranchised that you had so little say in any of the decisions?"

"Sure it bothered me, but I sort of got used to it. I learned how to treat Bernie so that he would not blow up. He has a horrible temper. I learned to adjust."

"And you were happy with the marriage then?"

"I wouldn't say happy. It was okay, I guess. Besides, what was there to do about it? There was no talking to Bernie. He would just explode if I said anything. He felt we had the ideal marriage and that everything was just peachy."

"Did you ever unburden yourself to your parents?"

"Are you kidding? The first week we were married Bernie laid down the law that I was never to talk to my parents about anything that went on in our lives, because that brings parents in to meddle, and meddling parents have broken up many families. In fact, Bernie objected even to my talking to my parents at all. [This is a strategy whereby the husband tries to isolate the wife.] I call my mother when he's at work, but he's got a nose like a bloodhound, and I don't know how he detects this. He will say, 'You talked to your mother today, didn't you? I can tell by the way you're talking that you've been talking with her. Well, you'd better stop that. She puts crazy ideas into your head. You are my wife, and you do things the way I want.'"

Shall we continue? The entire interview was a long litany of abusive behavior that began the first week of marriage and had fully escalated until it resulted in physical violence. Bella had suffered 19 years in an abusive relationship, feeling isolated and helpless. The more she felt powerless, the easier it was for her husband to make his domination of her even more absolute. All avenues for any kind of self-expression were closed off. More than a century after slavery was abolished, Bella was a slave to a despotic husband.

Bella did not see any options. After the incident when her husband was physically abusive, she gathered the courage to consult her rabbi, who greeted her with "Mrs. Segal! It is a pleasure to see you. Let me tell you, Mrs. Segal, your son Marvin is a jewel. Just like his father. You will have much *nachas* from him. He is a born leader just like Bernard. You know, your husband was just re-elected for the third time as president of the Men's Club. There was no question about it. When Bernard Segal is in charge, things get done. All our events have gone off without a single hitch. A wonderful man, your husband. You are fortunate to have a husband like him." Bella just mumbled a few words that she was just passing by the synagogue and had stopped in to say hello, and hurriedly left. What was she to do? Vilify the saint of the synagogue? The rabbi would never believe her.

So Bella was trapped. She was a non-person, just an appendage to her husband. When she was in the bathroom after the arm twisting, face slapping, and pushing incident and had looked at the bottle of pills, that was one of the rare occasions when she was thinking of doing something for herself. Yes, committing suicide would be for herself. But this was not an option either. The children needed a mother, and again, this time fortunately, Bella set herself aside. Bella existed only for others, but not for herself.

Well, so what? Isn't Jewish history replete with heroes who were self-sacrificing and accepted martyrdom out of conviction that they would rather die than renounce their faith? Why can't we consider Bella to be a hero, a self-sacrificing person who chose to set her own happiness aside in order to maintain the integrity of her family, to give her four children a home?

Wrong. Bella was not a hero, not a self-sacrificing martyr. *Bella was a victim.* Our heroes who died for their faith had the option of saving their lives by renouncing their faith and converting. They had a choice. Bella had no choice, or at least she felt she had no choice. Bella was trapped. She was not a martyr, Bella was a victim. [I know that there are some who object to the term "victim," but I do not know of a more appropriate term].

We might even question the wisdom of Bella's decision to keep the family intact in order to avoid negatively affecting her children. Even if the children did not witness either the verbal or physical abuse, is it not unrealistic to think they were not impacted upon by the attitude in the home? Would it really be a benefit to Marvin or to Stanley to grow up just like their father, and perhaps their wives would be as miserable as Bella? Or for Sandra and Esther to identify with a long-suffering mother and conclude that this is a woman's destiny in life, to suffer in silence?

This is most often the problem in the family where there is abuse. Resignation, hopelessness, despair. One must accept things and make the best of them, because there is just no way out. Nothing can be done to change things.

Is this really true?

If Bella had been more adequately prepared, she could have identified her husband's attempt to dominate and control her as emotional abuse. Many women do not think that it is wrong for the husband to have dictatorial control or to isolate them from the family or even to belittle and embarrass them. If Bella had been more knowledgeable about what is and what is not abuse, she might have made an educated decision about what to do. This would have been the golden opportunity to strengthen her and possibly to get her husband into counseling. It is conceivable that salutary changes could have been made that could have saved the marriage.

Chapter 2

Judaism and Domestic Abuse - Is There Immunity?

Does abuse ever occur in respectable families? That is, with professional people who have a strong work ethic, religious experience, people who do not drink or gamble and are in no other way antisocial? The answer is, yes. Abuse is non-discriminating, and may occur where it is least expected.

What about people who are devoutly religious and spiritual? Wait a moment. Let us not confuse terms. Truly spiritual people are very unlikely to be abusive, and truly devout religious people, who are wholesomely religious and observe *all* of Torah law are very unlikely to be abusive. You see, the Talmud states that the proper attitude of a husband toward his wife is that "He loves her as much as himself and honors her more than he honors himself" (*Yevamos* 62B). A person who is truly Torah observant adheres to *all* Talmudic requirements. Clearly, a person who loves his wife as himself and respects her even more than he does himself is very unlikely to be an abuser. The latter behavior is simply incompatible with true Torah observance.

The Biblical commandment "Love your neighbor as yourself" (*Leviticus* 19:18) and the Talmudic statement to love a wife as one loves himself presumes that a person does indeed love oneself. This is not universally true. As I pointed out in *Life's Too Short* (St. Martins Press, 1995) many people harbor negative feelings about themselves and do not like themselves. Indeed, the need to dominate and control may be a desperate defense against feelings of inadequacy and unworthiness which are generally unwarranted.

But if religious means a person who observes ritual law, even scrupulously, but neglects the ethical teachings of the Torah, then the answer is yes. Such a person may be an abuser.

An entire volume of the Talmud, *Ethics Of The Fathers*, is totally devoted to refinement of character traits. There are beautiful teachings of humility, of forgiveness, of generosity, of being slow to anger and easy to appease, of being respectful of others, of shunning personal glorification, of exerting control over oneself, of going out of one's way to avoid strife, of pursuing peace, of being pleasant to everyone, of avoiding rage, envy, and temptation, of minimizing indulgence in physical pleasures, of dedicating one's life to fulfilling the will of G-d rather than satisfying one's own will...and many, many more. These are all Torah teachings which a truly devout person must observe with the same fervor and dedication that he chooses kosher food or arranges for the observance of Shabbos. This, incidentally, is what is meant by spirituality, and there are many fine people who are diligent in trying to implement these Torah values in their lives.

The principles stated in *Ethics Of The Fathers* are further elucidated, expanded, and elaborated in many fine works on *midos* (character traits) that have been composed by Torah authorities throughout the ages. We are also privileged to have authentic accounts of the lives of men and women who practiced these ethical principles in their lives, and of whom it could be said, "A person who is looked upon favorably by other people is a person who is looked upon favorably by G-d" (*Ethics Of The Fathers* 3:10). "Looked upon favorably by other people" means by *all* other people, including one's wife and children. This type of truly wholesome, religious-spiritual behavior precludes abusing anyone, man, woman, or child.

We would be less than honest if we asserted that everyone who is meticulous in ritual law is equally committed to the demands of Torah ethics. We may know observant people who are lacking in humility and may become quite upset if they are not accorded the honor which they feel is their due, or who have a short fuse and are rather easily provoked to rage. There may be people who are distressed because they cannot equal the standard of living of some of their neighbors, and who may be envious of them. It is possible that a ritually observant person might say a cross word to his wife because she served a dish of which he is not enamored, whereas a highly spiritual person is one who eats only to provide the nourishment needed for existence, and who is not at all particular about gustatory delights. There is thus no assurance that because a person observes ritual law, that his character traits are impeccable.

What about a person who comes from a very loving home, whose parents have had a very stable marriage, and to all outward appearances, an ideal marriage. Ah! That last qualifying clause undoes everything: "To all outward appearances." Many families maintain a facade of perfect harmony, whereas behind closed doors there may be sheer havoc. One of the cardinal rules in a dysfunctional family is "Keep your silence. Nothing about what goes on in this house is ever to be made known outside of it." And you know what? The rule is observed. If the government bureaucracy were able to invoke a gag rule as efficiently as a dysfunctional family does, the problem of leaking sensitive information would be solved.

Neither race, religion, ethnic group, philosophical orientation, socioeconomic level, educational level...none of these preclude abuse. I have a reliable, personal communication from a woman who supervises the *mikvah* in a neighborhood in Israel that is largely Ashkenazic. She informed me that it is not all that uncommon to see women who have bruises, physical evidence of being battered, and who have confided this to her, but do not think there is anything they can do about it. There is simply no immunity.

That abuse can happen anywhere means that help must be available everywhere and for everyone. One of the goals of this book is to increase awareness of domestic abuse, so that more professional counselors and rabbis will take seriously the complaint of a woman whose husband is respected and esteemed, and not dismiss it as fantasy. Careful and sensitive investigation is essential to get at the truth, and a woman whose husband is an honorable person in the community should not be denied help.

If there is no immunity, what can one do to avoid entering a relationship with an abusive person? Are there any particular warning signals, things to look out for? Let us see.

Chapter 3

Warning Signs for Controlling Relationships

One of the weakest areas in human psychology is prediction of behavior. Psychiatrists are often asked to testify in court about a given person's potential for violent behavior. The track record of success in predicting behavior is nothing to write home about. The correlation of psychological profiles with actual occurrence or absence of subsequent violence is rather low, and the "hunch" of a non-professional is probably of equal reliability. About all one can say that has some statistical validity is that if a person has been violent once, he is more likely to be violent again than a person who has never manifested violent behavior, and it hardly takes a Ph.D. to make this astute observation.

Many attempts have been made, for example, to predict future alcoholism from a psychological profile, and these have all been non-productive. About all we can say is that the child of an alcoholic parent has a greater chance of becoming alcoholic than one where there was no familial alcoholism, and this propensity appears to be genetic. That is, children who were adopted at birth who had an alcoholic parent and were raised in a non-alcoholic home still have the same increased propensity to become alcoholic as those who were raised by a biological parent who was an alcoholic. It is also true that children who were raised in an abusive home have a greater likelihood of being abusers themselves, but there is no evidence for a genetic component. This appears to be a learned behavior.

It is rather unlikely that you would be able to base your romantic interests on a battery of psychological tests anyway. What would you do? "Hello? Yes, this is Barbara speaking...how nice of you to call, but before I would consider meeting you, I would like to have a copy of your MMPI and Rorschach. Notarized, please." Not too much chance of your doing that. But don't feel bad about it. Neither the MMPI or the Rorschach are reliable predictors of abuse.

There are, however, at least some behavioral clues which are red flags. Mind you, they are not *predictors* of abuse, but they do indicate a higher risk. Here are some risk factors:

(1) Someone who was emotionally or physically abused as a child.

(2)A person whose father was an abuser.

(3) A person who has behaved violently toward others.

(4) A person who loses his temper more frequently and more easily than others.

(5) A person who breaks things when angry.

(6) A person who uses alcohol to excess. (Many abusers do not drink, but a person who drinks excessively may lose control more easily)

The following are warning signs:

(1) Does he try to isolate you from family and friends?

(2) Does he expect you to spend all your free time with him exclusively?

(3)Does he want to know your whereabouts all the time and becomes angry when you are not available? (These three traits may be misinterpreted as intense love, whereas they may actually be an attempt to control).

(4)Is he very impatient? For example, does he get angry in a restaurant if the service is not what he wants, then perhaps blame you for wanting to eat there?

(5)Does he become angry if you do not follow his advice?

(6)Does he take responsibility for his own actions, or is he always blaming others?

(7)Does he tend to put you down, and you discover that you are putting yourself down in order to please him?

(8)Does he appear to have two sides to his personality?

(9)Is he ever cruel, or on the other hand, smothering with excessive kindness?

(10)Are you afraid of making him angry and so take great caution not to do so?

(11)Does he have unrealistic expectations of you as a wife and/or mother?

A man may have one or more of these traits or warning signs and not turn out to be an abuser. All we are saying is that any of these traits increase the risk of potentially abusive and controlling behavior.

In that segment of the population where marriages are arranged by *shidduchim* (matchmaking) and where the young man and woman do not meet often prior to their wedding, even these alerting signals are unavailable. While parents do try to find out as much as they can about a young man's character and family of origin from friends and teachers, this information is rather limited. Some of this behavior may not have been seen in either the school or social setting, and if there are any skeletons in the closet, they are quite likely to remain well concealed. Incidentally, it is important to inquire whether the young man is kind, respectful to other people, and considerate of others' feelings. Careful questioning may elicit important data about a person. Also, while there is frequently adequate research about the family's financial and social standing it is far more important to try and to find out something meaningful about the husband's attitude toward the wife. For example, if it is found out that the father frequently helps the mother do the dishes, it is a much more significant factor in the young man's favor than the father's earnings.

The *shidduch* system has the advantage of avoiding many psychological incompatibilities. A young man and a young woman from very different backgrounds and with markedly discordant value systems may "fall in love" and in their state of infatuation, may ignore the major differences which may be the cause of incompatibility when the infatuation stage is over. The alignment of two people from similar backgrounds and values that is achieved by the *shidduch* system avoids this particular pitfall. Some rabbis have recommended the *shidduch* system as a filtering technique for introductory purposes, but that there should be more frequent dating and a better chance of observing the person prior to making a commitment to marry. It is characteristic of controlling men that they insist the girl make a quick decision. Undue pressure may be a warning sign.

While this recommendation appears to be most sensible, one should consider that many marriages that were preceded by extensive courtship have nevertheless resulted in abuse.

Firstly, there is the infatuation factor. A young woman who has stars in her eyes may see her beau as her prince charming, hero, and protector. The warning signals could be flashed to her with bright neon lights, and she would not see them. This is a fact of life: People do not see what they do not want to see. I have dealt with a number of cases where parents, who were not affected by the young man's charms alerted the daughter to some character traits that caused them great concern, but she dismissed these with, "You don't know him as well as I." The young woman may not be able to see these character defects, just as the Torah says "A bribe will blind the eyes of the wise" (*Deuteronomy* 16:19), and a young woman who is "bribed" by a young man's charms may be blinded to his defects. This does not mean that parents are always right, but neither are they always wrong. By the same token, when a girl is not favorably inclined toward the young man, parents should take this seriously and not push her into marriage because they think the young man is ideal.

Another reason why warning signals may be ineffective is that even if they are noted, a young woman may say, "He is going to change for me," or "I know I can change him." To this young woman I say, "If you wish to marry a man who smokes or drinks or gambles, that is your constitutional right, and no one can stop you. But if you object to any of these behaviors and think for one moment that you are going to change someone, *forget it! What you see is what you get,* and do not deceive yourself that it is going to be otherwise.

I cannot tell you how many wives of alcoholics who bewail their plight tell me that their father was an alcoholic. When I ask whether they knew their husband drank excessively prior to their marriage, they say, "Yes." "Then why on earth did you marry him?" I ask. The answer: "I thought I could change him." What is even more amazing is that if they divorce this alcoholic husband, the odds are that they will marry another alcoholic, using the same or another rationalization.

Thirdly, abusive behavior may occur in the absence of any early warning signs. The abusive aspect of the man's personality might not be manifested until after the relationship is securely sealed by the marriage contract. The abuser may then feel himself legally empowered to dominate, and to dominate absolutely. It is as though the marriage license is an instrument authorizing tyranny and abuse. If the wife is financially dependent on him, this only increases his feelings of power and control. As she becomes more dependent when she has one or more children, and particularly in a legal/social system where she is at a disadvantage and is unprotected if she were to try to leave the marriage, the sensation of mastery may increase. At any point along this spectrum of inflation of power, emotional or physical abuse may emerge.

Finally, a young woman who was raised in an abusive home may assume that this is the normal way of life. While she may be able to recognize physical violence as abuse, she may not be able to identify some of the early warning signals that are indications of a propensity for emotional abuse, since she has seen her mother adjust to this. She may accept male tyranny as the way the world was meant to be. In this way, abuse is perpetuated both by sons who adopt a father's abusive behavior and daughters who adopt the mother's resignation.

If there is no certain way of identifying a potential abuser, what can a woman do? The answer is *be alert for if and when it happens.* In the absence of actual prevention, the next best thing is *early case identification.* In the overwhelming number of wife-abuse cases, the woman has been tolerating abuse for years by the time she finally seeks help from anyone. This is wrong, dead wrong. Abuse should be nipped in the bud.

Chapter 4

Early Case Identification

I must take issue with any authority who defines a battered wife as one who has been beaten for a second time, yet continues to stay in the marriage. I disagree. *Once is once too often.* There is no justification, except for the rare case of when a woman would be attacking her husband, for a husband to ever be physically aggressive towards his wife. It is a serious error to overlook a first incident. There is no grace period. If a husband is physically abusive to his wife even once, the wife should promptly seek counsel.

It is not too much different in the case of emotional abuse, except that physical abuse is easier to define. A hostile push, a slap, a twisted arm, forced sex, are all physical abuse. Emotional abuse, while of no less gravity, needs a bit of definition. Not every husband-wife argument comprises emotional abuse, and while screaming, use of profane language, or saying "shut up!" are to be condemned, a single such episode is not necessarily emotional abuse. However, if the wife says, as she should, "Gene, I am not going to be talked to like that. I don't ever wish to hear that tone of voice or words like that used against me, not ever again," and if there is nevertheless a repetition of such verbal insults, that does constitute emotional abuse. It is an indication that the husband does not respect his wife's right to be treated with dignity, and such inconsiderate behavior is sufficient reason for her to seek help. *This does not mean that a single episode of physical or emotional abuse is reason to terminate the relationship,* but it is reason enough to seek competent counseling.

Yes, we are told to emulate G-d and to be kind, considerate, and forgiving. But one must have an understanding of what one is dealing with. There can be ill-advised forgiveness which amounts to "enabling." That is, if the person who is abusive sees that his behavior is being tolerated, it encourages repetition and progression of this behavior, and when this occurs, the tolerance actually feeds into the abusive behavior. The abuser must be stopped in his tracks, and the issue looked at frankly and as objectively as possible. Countless women have jeopardized their lives by hoping that a breast lump will melt away on its own. Fortunately, sometimes it does, but when it does not, each day it is permitted to exist increases the risk of grave disease. Abuse must be looked at as a malignant condition. If it can be totally extirpated, life can continue normally. This requires early diagnosis, and a woman should not delude herself with false hopes that the abusive behavior is going to fade away.

There is a psychological mechanism known as **denial** which is essentially an unconscious process that shuts off a person's awareness of something whose recognition poses a threat. The analogy of a breast lump, is again valid. Some women will not perform routine breast examination for fear that they may discover a lump, and they operate on the erroneous assumption that "what you don't know won't hurt you." This is as untrue of abuse as it is of a breast mass. What you don't know and what you choose to ignore, whether wittingly or unwittingly **can** hurt you a great deal.

"Well, yes, he did strike me once two years earlier, but I'm partially to blame for that. I said things that hurt him and he just lost his composure. He apologized profusely and said he didn't know what got into him, and said it will never happen again, and it didn't for the next two years."

For heaven's sake, my dear woman, stop justifying abuse! Stop blaming yourself. Even if you did provoke him, he is, or should be, a mature adult who can control his impulses. Nothing "got into him", *it was there all the time*, and it just became evident under these circumstances. What can be justified in a 5-year old cannot be justified in a 25-year old.

The denial of a breast mass is fueled by the anticipation of what might follow from an unfavorable diagnosis: surgery, body deformity, possibly radiation and chemotherapy--all things one wishes to avoid, and the fear of such eventualities is enough to block the awareness of the mass. Similarly with abuse, if it is overlooked and forgotten about, then life can continue "normally," whereas if one recognizes the problem, there is the possibility of confrontation and therapy, discovering incompatibilities, perhaps separation, loss of financial support, social embarrassment, and possibly even provoking more abuse as a reaction. All these dreaded conditions may militate to bring about a denial of the problem.

Unfortunately, denial only allows the unattended problem to fester, and very much like a dormant volcano, there may be an eruption which will make denial impossible.

Esther did seek consultation three years after her marriage to Danny following an incident of his being physically rough, which was superimposed on a pattern of total domination. Danny had apologized and assured Esther it would never happen again. Esther did not feel that she was in danger of further physical violence, but was concerned about the emotional abuse. She was advised to get into counseling, which she did. The counseling did reveal some very major problems in the relationship. Inasmuch as physical violence did not appear to be a concern, separation was not felt to be necessary, but ongoing counseling for both Danny and Esther individually and later in conjoint therapy was recommended. Danny refused.

Esther was told that Danny's refusal to participate was ominous and she should begin preparing herself to be able to survive independently if it should come to that. She could take her parents into her confidence, and perhaps take courses that could give her a marketable skill if she needed to become financially self-sufficient. She was advised to avoid becoming pregnant until the stability of the marriage was assured.

Six years later, Esther again consulted me. While there had not been any recurrence of physical violence, the emotional abuse had persisted and escalated. Esther felt that she was no longer able to tolerate the hell she was in, and now wanted out of the marriage. She had not shared anything with her parents, had not acquired any marketable skills, and now had three children and was pregnant with the fourth. Danny's grip on Esther's life had been tightened, and her denial of the problem had allowed this to occur. What could have been done with less difficulty six years earlier was now a much more arduous task.

Some problems may be safely ignored in the hope they will go away, but problems like a breast mass or abuse, which have a potential for escalation, dare not be ignored. The price we pay for denial may be prohibitive.

Chapter 5

The Cyclic Pattern of Abuse

A number of counselors in the abuse field have reported what appears to be a fairly common pattern of abusive behavior, although there is great variation among cases. This is referred to as the "cyclic theory of violence," with a cycle that is comprised of three phases: (1) the tension-building phase, (2) the battering incident, and (3) the "honeymoon" phase.

Phase one is often initiated by varying degrees of oppression and control. The wife realizes what kinds of things may provoke her husband's anger, and may try to placate him by being compliant, anticipating his every whim, or perhaps just staying out of his way. In order for her to be able to maintain this attitude, she tries to avoid getting angry with her husband and may rationalize his oppressive behavior, often feeling that she is indeed somehow at fault.

In spite of her best efforts, there is a progressive increase of tension in both the wife and the husband. Her efforts at suppressing and denying her anger lose their effectiveness, while on the other hand, the abusive husband may actually become angrier because of her apparent passive acceptance of his behavior. Also, he may fear that she may become disgusted with him and leave, which causes him to become more jealous and possessive in the hope that he will keep her captive.

In an attempt to avert being hurt, the wife may try to eliminate as many irritating factors as possible. For example, if she fears that her family members may say or do something that will provoke the husband's rage, she may try to avoid such contacts, thus essentially increasing the isolation which the husband has initiated. Attempts to eliminate external provocations often only serve to delay but not eliminate the actual battering. During this tension-building phase there may be physical abuse such as pushing and shoving, and often increased verbal abuse, with name calling and humiliation.

The tension-building phase may last for months or even years, eventually giving rise to the explosive discharge.

It is little wonder that during the tension-building phase the woman may experience many symptoms, both physical and emotional. Anxiety, depression, insomnia, loss of appetite are common, or just the reverse, overeating, over-sleeping, and fatigue. Women are also likely to have frequent headaches, digestive complaints, skin reactions, and palpitations. Even if they should seek professional help for these symptoms, they are unlikely to reveal the source of their problem.

Phase two, the actual battering incident is characterized by an uncontrollable discharge of the tensions that had been building up. The husband may begin his violence under the impression that he "only wants to teach his wife a lesson," but loses control of his behavior and may inflict very serious injury. During the actual battering the woman may feel completely helpless and may do nothing to resist. She may feel that any kind of resistance will only provoke greater violence, and some women have reported that they tried to remain calm and let the storm pass, with the belief that things will be better once it is over with.

Many battered women do not seek help immediately following the attack unless they are so severely injured that they go to a hospital emergency room. They generally return home to the husband who had inflicted the injuries.

Phase three, the "honeymoon" phase, ushers in an unusual period of calm, with the batterer exhibiting kindness and contrite, loving behavior. He expresses his regret for having lost control and attacking her, begging his wife's forgiveness and promising that he will never do it again. He may cry bitterly and wallow in remorse. He may actually believe that he will never again hurt the wife whom he loves so dearly and that henceforth he will control himself. He may also feel that he has "taught her a lesson" and there will therefore not be any further provocation to such behavior. He may try to convince his wife of his remorse and sincerity by giving up types of behavior that displease her. It is also fairly common for the husband to now buy gifts for his wife, even some which he cannot afford.

The battered wife desperately wants to believe that the abuse is over, and that the husband has indeed turned a new leaf. He appears so sincere in his desire to change that she convinces herself that he will indeed keep his promise. He may again become the "prince charming" of their courtship. It is characteristic that at this phase the woman will drop charges, back down on steps toward a separation, and even try to patch things up between her husband and her family. The husband may convince the wife how desperately he needs her, and that if she would leave him he would have a "nervous breakdown" or commit suicide. The woman may begin to see herself as holding the key to her husband's emotional health, and feel responsible for his well being.

There is great variation on how long phase three lasts, but insidiously, the contrition wears away, and the next tension-building phase begins.

Almost invariably, the wife sees the considerate, loving behavior of phase three as being the "true" personality of her husband, while phases one and two, although they may exceed phase three in duration, are alien to him.

Women who finally come for help have generally gone through several such cycles. Each cycle diminishes the woman's self-esteem, making her progressively more vulnerable to increased abuse.

Chapter 6

Denial In The Jewish Community

In our discussion of early case identification, we mentioned the phenomenon of **denial**, wherein a person's mind effectively shuts off the awareness of something, where such awareness is perceived as threatening. We cited the classic example of a woman who refuses to examine her breasts for fear that she might discover a lump, and we compared this to the woman who refuses to recognize that her husband is an abuser. Denial is an unconscious mechanism, and seems to operate on the principle that it is better not to know something bad, and that if you ignore it, it will go away.

Denial is as true of a group and of a community as it is of an individual. There are many instances when a large group of people ignore the obvious, as, for example, when many German Jews were unable to see the forthcoming danger in the years of Hitler's rise to power, and never gave a thought that they might lose everything they had. There is denial in the medical and psychiatric communities, as I discovered in retrospect, that in my four years of medical school and three years of psychiatric training I did not receive a single lecture, not one morsel of knowledge about alcoholism, drug addiction, and spousal abuse. This unfortunate situation has resulted in many doctors failing to detect these conditions, and not knowing what to do if they did detect one of them.

The Jewish community has been and still is in denial of the presence of some social problems in its midst. We have long cherished the belief that "*shikker is a goy*" and have refused to consider the possibility that alcoholism may be at the root of many problems. We have also cherished the belief that Jewish husbands are angels, always caring, kind, and considerate, and that it is unthinkable for a Jewish husband to knowingly harm his wife.

It is difficult to know whether these were always myths or whether they were true at one time. There is reason to believe that Jewish life in the shtetl was much different from that in modern America. Living under oppression draws people closer to one another, as they close ranks in the interest of survival. It has happened repeatedly that when under attack from a common enemy, people who were sworn adversaries bonded together in a single-minded purpose. It is likely that when Jews were disenfranchised and persecuted, no one could afford the luxury of internal strife, and this may have prevented discord within the family as well. The Jewish couple could ill afford any internal dissention, and it may well be that this was the source of the belief that the Jewish family is a bulwark of solidarity and that Jewish husbands are not batterers. Thus, it may have been true at one time. All this notwithstanding, there were incidents of wife abuse. One prominent rabbi, when asked if there were such cases in the old country, said, "Yes, but people closed the shutters so that no one would hear."

As Jews Americanized and enjoyed the rights and privileges of their non-Jewish neighbors; as they became doctors and lawyers and college professors and successful businessmen; as the danger from hostile neighbors appeared to diminish, this unifying force was attenuated, and as the need for strong family bonds weakened, more Jewish husbands became abusive. But, myths die hard, particularly when we very much wish to believe them, and so we have hung on to the idea that Jewish husbands cannot be batterers. When facts to the contrary began to become evident, we just refused to see them. When wife abuse does occur in the Jewish family, the denial that is so characteristic of the condition among women of all ethnic groups is reinforced many times over by the denial in the Jewish community.

A couple may consult their rabbi because of problems in the marriage, and the rabbi is likely to inquire about financial difficulties or other factors that may cause stress in the home, and is particularly apt to focus on *in-law* problems, since Jewish parents are so often thought to be meddlers. However, it is most unlikely that the rabbi will inquire about whether there has been any battering. It simply does not occur to him to pose this question any more than it would occur to him that perhaps the sun rose in the west, and if he does pose it, he may do so in the presence of the abuser, so that the wife cannot answer truthfully. Furthermore, if the wife had intended to bring this up, the unspoken taboo that is conveyed by the rabbi's attitude effectively silences her.

In the rather unlikely event that the wife were to mention that she has been physically abused, the husband is likely to minimize it. "All I did was push her out of the way," he will say. He may even go on to say, "I'm sorry I did even that. She had provoked me, and I happened to be very exhausted and irritable after a grueling day at the office, and I just lost my cool momentarily. But that will never happen again." The rabbi, who is not only a believer in the myth, but also an advocate of **teshuva** and that sincere remorse eradicates even the gravest sins, readily accepts the husband's account and promise, and the issue of battering is dismissed. The wife, who had finally broken through her own denial now has it reinstated by the rabbi, and we are back to square one. The woman may never reach out again. Any subsequent counseling may evade this central issue, and nothing is accomplished.

If this is true of physical abuse, it is even more so of emotional or verbal abuse. So what if a husband raises his voice occasionally? Even insults and derogatory comments are dismissed as insignificant. The important thing is to bring peace and harmony back to the family, especially for the sake of the children. "Let's forget about the mistakes of the past, wipe the slate clean, and start again. Let's bring back the love and mutual attraction that brought you together and begin a new phase with the second honeymoon."

It all sounds so pleasant, so ideal. We so wish it to be true that we convince ourselves that it will be true. Everyone leaves the rabbi's study in high spirits, the couple feeling rejuvenated in their love, (or the woman terrified) and the rabbi, feeling that he has performed his duties well and has reinstated **shalom bayis** (peace within the home), the greatest of all the *mitzvos.*

Restoring **shalom bayis** is indeed a great *mitzvah*, but there is also a scriptural command "Do not stand by and see your neighbor's blood spilled" (*Leviticus* 19:16), which the Talmud interprets to mean that one is obligated to ward off any harm that may occur to another person. It requires much skill and sensitivity to know when to do what. Failing to address the issue of wife abuse properly and sending a woman back to suffer at the hands of a controlling husband is not preserving **shalom bayis**. *An abusive husband who has the need to dominate and control his wife is not going to change because he gave his word to the rabbi.* This is a delusion of which we must divest ourselves.

I was inadequately prepared both as a rabbi and as a psychiatrist to recognize and deal with many of the real problems both in my congregation and among my patients. It is incumbent upon rabbinical seminaries to include courses on the various social conditions in their curricula, and upon rabbinical organizations to arrange for post-graduate seminars to acquaint rabbis to the facts of life and give them a thorough understanding of these problems. There are professional counselors who will provide the necessary training.

A woman is unlikely to divulge information about abuse in the presence of her husband for fear of retaliation. When a couple comes to the rabbi with a problem in the marriage, it is important that the rabbi see them individually as well, and ask, "Is there anything that you were hesitant to tell me in the presence of your husband/wife?" The statement "Jack is really a good-hearted soul and a very devoted father" may well be a cue, but the wife cannot bring herself to say "But at times he becomes so enraged that I don't recognize him. He is like two different people." Sensitivity to the wife's guarded statements would enable the rabbi to say what the wife cannot. "Even good-hearted people sometimes say and do things that are out of character for them. Has Jack ever been unkind to you?" Better have a box of kleenex ready, because you may have opened the door to an ocean of feelings that have been dammed behind the floodgates.

While social workers in Jewish family agencies are apt to be more alert to the problem of wife abuse than rabbis, there is still need for continuing education in this area. There may be resistances to thoroughly investigating the possibility of wife abuse. It can be frustrating and exhausting, and a lack of awareness of the intensity of denial may allow a social worker to be falsely assured by an initial response, "Oh, never. My husband would never lay a finger on me." I have seen women with broken bones say that. Furthermore, the possibility of emotional abuse may be easily overlooked.

The Jewish community needs to come to grips with this problem. What are the statistics? How widespread is this problem? No one knows, and there can be no reliable estimate of a problem which is so densely concealed. Suffice it to say that the incidence of the problem is greater than what we may think, and even if it is true that it is less than in the non-Jewish population, that is a hollow consolation. It is still far too great an incidence, and it is the responsibility of the community to do whatever it can to remedy it and provide resources for help.

Denial takes on yet another form. It reminds me of the reluctant alcoholic, who, under pressure, admits he has a drinking problem, whereby he means to say, "Okay, I've admitted it. You got what you wanted, now get off my back." This "confession" is just another variety of denial and avoidance of dealing with the problem.

Some communities have organized public lectures, with a speaker or panel, and these may be well attended. Having brought it into the open with such a forum, the job has been done. Everyone in the audience shakes his head sadly, "Tsk, tsk. How terrible!", and then everyone goes home and minds their own business.

In no way do I mean to minimize the importance of public lectures. They make a significant contribution by exposing a problem that has been so tightly concealed and defended. For some people, such lectures are the first chance to even hear about wife abuse in the Jewish community. Public lectures may stimulate a community to take steps to provide for the needs of the abused wife.

However, let us not lose sight of the fact that an abused wife does not get any relief from public lectures, and the latter must be translated into action. The abused wife needs help, real help. Every Jewish community should have a 24-hour hotline, operated by trained personnel.

There should be immediate access to legal counsel* provided by the community, proper shelter accommodations provided for the wife and children, and emergency funds for temporary support until something can be worked out. There needs to be trained staff to help these women with realistic decisions. There need to be rabbis who

---

*Torah law requires recourse to a Beth Din (Rabbinical Court) and not to secular courts or police. The exception to this is when one is threatened by violence, when it is permissible to call for police protection if one has no other way of protecting oneself.

can help in ways we shall soon discuss. There needs to be a network of supportive people, especially women who have survived abuse and have gone through the "University of Experience." These services cost money, and the community has the obligation to see that they are adequately funded. Too often community services receive token funding, and some agencies cannot meet a fraction of the demand for services. Funding must be realistic.

Every possible method must be implemented to protect the woman from the batterer. Orders of protection, while necessary and helpful, are by no means a guarantee of safety.

One tactic which has not received adequate use is that of social pressure. The ancients knew this, and the use of *herem* or excommunication was a potent behavioral restraint. It was then and can be now.

Herem is more than a religious injunction. Human beings are social creatures, and being deprived of relating to other people can be a powerful sanction. A person who is known to be a wife-abuser but who is welcomed in the synagogue, given an *aliyah* to the Torah, and accorded other privileges takes this as a confirmation that he is really "a nice guy", and that the community recognizes that his wife is the problematic person. A known wife abuser should be informed that unless he avoids all abusive behavior, and unless he takes corrective measures–not promises–to overcome his abusiveness, he will be publicly excommunicated. He will not receive any privileges in the synagogue, no one will greet him, let alone converse and transact with him, and he will be ostracized from the community. While this may not be equally effective with everyone, there are situations where this social pressure will help restrain abuse and encourage a recalcitrant husband to meet his obligations to his wife and children and to seek help for his problem.

As with the alcohol or drug problem, denial of the presence of wife abuse among Jews may not be overcome until it strikes close to home. One Jewish organization was asked to provide a slot for discussion of wife abuse on its convention agenda, but the person in charge of the agenda said it was not an item of high priority. One year later he called to offer his apologies, his daughter and her two children having just come back home to get away from a battering husband.

If we overcome the denial in the community now, we may be spared the distress of coming to our senses when our daughters identify themselves as victims of batterers.

Chapter 7

Why Did She Stay With Him?

This is perhaps the question people ask most frequently when hearing of an account of a woman who was repeatedly battered. While it is a logical question which deserves an answer, it may also betray a cultural attitude, i.e., that the woman who was the victim of the battering actually contributed to her misery by not leaving the relationship earlier. In a way, this places blame on the woman instead of on the man who committed the criminal assault.

This is not an unusual occurrence. We seem to have a tendency to blame the victim. There are those who hold the victim of rape responsible as though she had seduced the rapist. The question "Why did she not leave him" seems to accept the batterer as a given, as though nothing can be done about him, which then makes the wife's leaving the only apparent solution to the problem. Perhaps if the focus were on making certain that the batterer did not have an opportunity to repeat his assault, there would be no reason for the woman to leave.

When listening to an account by an abused wife, it is common to hear her say, "When it happened at first I was upset, but I didn't panic. Although he did hurt me, I felt I could change him. It wasn't until much later that I realized that he was set in his ways."

Because of the frequency of this attitude early in the course of abuse, I must reiterate that it is a serious mistake for a woman to think that she is going to change her husband. It's about time we stopped filling our young children's impressionable minds with stories about a beautiful princess who kisses a frog and turns him into a charming prince. For women who think they can change their husbands I say,

"You will not change a frog into a prince, nor an abuser into a non-abuser."

I do not mean to imply that a person cannot change. *Change can occur if the person himself so wishes, and such change will come about if he recognizes that he has a need to change, but change can be only by the person's **own** effort. You, the wife, cannot change him.* Nor is there any value in the promise of an abuser never again to repeat his actions, anymore than there is in the promise of an alcoholic that he will never drink again. The behavior that elicits such promises may have been traumatic and destructive and the alcoholic or abuser may manifest such profound remorse that their sincerity appears unquestionable. Experience has taught us that neither remorse nor promises have any reliability whatsoever.

Let us now turn to the question, Why would a woman stay with an abuser? Why doesn't she simply up and leave? The answer is because there is no "simply up and leave." Our social structure has not provided a battered wife with conditions that would facilitate her leaving.

Firstly, she and her children are likely to be totally or largely dependent on her husband's earnings. Who will support them if she leaves? Recourse to the courts for support is not satisfactory. There are many deadbeat fathers who do not support their families.

Secondly, where are she and the children to go? She has a furnished home, where she and her children have their rooms and all of their belongings. She may be able to reside temporarily in the shelter (if the community she lives in has one), but obviously a shelter is not a permanent residence.

Let us suppose that she is able to relocate away from her husband. Many batterers are vengeful, and have carried out their threats to find the wife and kill her. Is she to live in constant fear that her husband may show up at any moment and hurt or kill her? You may suggest that she obtain a court injunction or order a protection barring the husband from contacting her. Let me inform you that many women have been killed by the battering husband in spite of their being in possession of an order of protection.

Fourth, society may not look favorably upon a woman who leaves her husband. She was supposed to "preserve the family unit," and she may feel that she is a deserter. Also, she thinks (and rightly so) that no one will believe her. In any number of cases, a woman has fled to the asylum of her parent's home, only to have them urge her to return, because "the children need a father." The ignorance that abounds about behavior of an abuser is alarming, and well-meaning but unknowledgeable parents have sent their daughter to her doom.

Fifth, in some cultures, such as the Orthodox community where marriages are initiated by a *shidduch* (matchmaking) a young man or woman from a home where there was known to be abuse may not be considered favorably for a *shidduch.* Knowledge in the community of significant discord within the home may stigmatize the children, hence the penchant for secrecy. One woman, the mother of nine children, of whom the oldest three were married, stated that her youngest child was seven years old, and that she must remain in an abusive relationship for the next 12 years until this youngest child is married. For her to leave the marriage would be to stigmatize the children, and she felt that having brought the children into the world, she has the responsibility to protect them from stigma, and to avoid setting up obstacles to their happiness. She was therefore resigned to tolerate 12 more years of torment! It should be apparent that the husband, well aware of this attitude, feels himself empowered to behave as he wishes, since he knows that his wife cannot do anything to thwart his behavior.

The latter point is true throughout. The many factors that make it unrealistic for an abused woman to leave also reinforce the abuser, who feels there is no restraint to his absolute domination.

Sixth, the abused woman may have become so totally crushed that she may lack the confidence to do anything in her own behalf. Even if the means for independent existence were technically present, she may not have the emotional strength to take the initiative to leave.

Seventh, a woman may stay in an abusive relationship because she is afraid that the husband will take the children from her. Controlling husbands may flex their legal muscle and convince the wife that she has no chance of having the children if she leaves.

Eighth, even if the woman is assured that she would have custody of the children, she may feel that it is better to maintain the relationship because, "My children deserve a father," or "They love him." While there is no denying that a wholesome marriage which provides children with two caring parents is ideal and is most conducive to the children's emotional well-being, it should also be realized that there may be serious psychological damage to the children who witness an ongoing abusive relationship.

Finally, it is not uncommon for an abused woman to actually justify the abusive behavior. How often have I heard, "I thought I was doing something wrong. I felt I deserved it." This feeling, while totally unrealistic, results in total self-effacement, with the woman becoming a non-person, which is exactly what the abusing husband wishes.

In Torah there is the concept of community responsibility. If a person is found murdered and the assailant is unknown, the elders and leaders of the nearest community must declare, "Our hands did not spill this blood" (*Deuteronomy* 21). This requires a thorough self-searching, and the Talmud states that the community leaders must investigate whether the crime may not have been the result of dereliction by the community to provide for the victim's welfare.

Some of the reasons why a woman cannot leave an abusive husband are due to the community's failure to make this more realistic, in which case it is not the woman who is at fault for not leaving the batterer, but the community for not making it more feasible.

Certainly the family, and especially parents, should be a prime resource for an abused wife. The decision to leave the husband, even temporarily, should not be made capriciously, but when adequate counseling and consideration result in such a decision, the woman should have the support of the family and the community.

Chapter 8

What the Torah Says About Abuse (I)

Wife abuse, whether physical or emotional, does not occur in a vacuum. It occurs in a society or culture which condones it, where male dominance is the norm, which subsumes male superiority and male despotism. It occurs in a society or culture where a woman is thought of as an inferior being, whose role is to make the life of males more pleasurable and more comfortable.

It is understandable why attitudes like this led to a feminist rebellion. The feminist movement is no different from any revolution of people who are oppressed and enslaved. The dignity of a human being lies in his being free, and deprivation of freedom is not only morally wrong, it is inhumane.

The tragedy is that the corrective measures implemented by the feminist movement, even if the latter has brought about some degree of emancipation, have not resulted in a significant decrease in the wife abuse problem. Women acquired the right to vote in 1911, and after this major breakthrough, elevation of the status of women proceeded at a snail's pace until the latter half of the 20th century, at which time the movement picked up momentum. Yet, the available statistics for the 20 years between 1975-1995 show a significant **increase** in the incidence of wife abuse. We might argue that the feminist movement is still in its infancy, and that it takes more than 40 years for significant social change to take root and bear fruit. It may also be argued that the increase in incidence is more apparent than real, and that the statistics reflect more accurate reporting, thanks to the elimination of the coverup that prevailed in a totally male-dominant society. All this notwithstanding, there is reason to believe that the gains achieved by women have not appreciably diminished the incidence of wife abuse.

There are terms which have acquired an air of sanctity and have become sacred cows, so sacred and supreme that one does not dare challenge them. "Equality" and "Democracy" are such sacred cows. While discrimination and oppression are unqualified evils, it does not follow that equality and democracy are the salvation of mankind. Even the concept of "separate but equal" has an opprobrium, as though anything other than absolute sameness in everything is the only acceptable lifestyle.

Torah does not posit absolute sameness, nor does nature. Men and women are different, and it is delusional to think otherwise. But different does not have to connote superior or inferior, better or worse, unless one wishes to interpret it that way.

Democracy may appear to be the most equitable way of government, although in the history of nations, the American experiment has not been around long enough to prove itself, and some major flaws in the system are quite evident. The worship of democracy and the attempt to impose it on all peoples of the world may not be the noble achievement we think it to be.

At any rate, the family is not a nation, and a family cannot operate by democratic principles. If the latter were true, children could outvote the parents and meals would consist of ice cream, chocolate, popcorn, pretzels and potato chips. School would be eliminated and the day would be spent eating cotton candy at the zoo or circus, and playing in the park, and bedtime would be whenever the kids were so exhausted that they dropped off to sleep on the living room floor.

It is also not realistic for there not to be a "titular" head of the family. The buck must stop somewhere, and any institution where there is equal responsibility and division of authority in top management is likely to be fraught with confusion and mismanagement.

The Midrash states that at the beginning of creation, the sun and the moon were of equal brightness, whereupon the moon complained to G-d, "Two kings cannot share one crown." G-d replied, "You are right, therefore you shall be the lesser of the two." We shall return to this Midrash a bit later, but its message is clear: the authority of management must rest in a CEO (Chief Executive Officer), and management by two coequals is inept and inefficient.

The logical question that you may ask is, "Okay, then why the male?" If it were the woman who were the titular head, the question would be the other way around. Then why not have a rotation? Come now, haven't you seen governments where rotation was tried and failed miserably? Are any of the successful corporations operated by a rotation of CEO's, whether for purpose of gender equality or any other reason? A corporation has a function, and maximum efficiency in achieving that function is with one titular head, one CEO. Can you imagine the chaos in a family if every now and then the titular head of the family would change?

Inasmuch as either one could have been given the position, how and why did the male get it? The Torah states that it was a consequence of Eve's being the first to transgress the Divine Word. Anthropologists may attribute the emergence of male dominance to the physically greater strength of the male. But we are missing the point completely if we become preoccupied with the male role as titular head of the family, because at least as far as Torah is concerned, *it was not intended to be a position of power.* This is stated clearly in the Midrash, which comments on the verse in *Genesis* 3:16 "He shall rule over you," saying: "This does *not* mean absolute rule. A man dare not harm his wife" (*Bereishis Rabbah*

20:18). The commentaries on this Midrash state that this understanding is derived from the sequence of verses in *Deuteronomy* 24:5-6. When a man marries a woman, he is exempt from military service for the first year so that he can provide companionship for her (24:5), and "he shall not harm" (24:6), which is, according to the Midrash, a Scriptural prohibition against wife abuse. A husband who injures his wife in any way is liable for damages, and even if there were no intent of harm, the principle that a person is always responsible for his actions and must pay for accidental injury, applies to the wife as well (*Choshen Mishpat* 421:12).

Halachic and ethical writings are emphatic on the prohibition of wife beating. Rabenu Jonah places this prohibition on an equal par with other Scriptural prohibitions (*Shaare Teshuva* 3:77). Rabbi Moses Isserles in the *Shulchan Aruch* states, "It is a sin for a man to beat his wife, and if he does this habitually the court can punish him, excommunicate him and whip him and apply all measures of force until he takes an oath never to do so again. If he violates this oath he may be compelled to divorce her" (*Even Hoezer* 154:3). Rabbi Mordechai ben Hillel, a halachic authority of the Middle Ages writes ". . . as with another person whom one is commanded not to beat. . . even more so with one's wife, whom one is obliged to honor more than one's own self"(Mordechai, *Kessubos* 185). The Chassidic master Rabbi Nachman of Breslau expressed the opprobrium of wife beatings as follows "If one spends all one's murderous anger upon her, shames her, raises one's hand to her–G-d forbid–the Almighty will demand recompense of him."

There are a number of cases in the responsa of husbands who insulted, degraded and threatened their wives, and this is sharply condemned.

The function of titular head of a family should not be confused with superiority or wielding control, and it is the

usurpation of superiority and control by males that has resulted in wife abuse.

Let me digress a moment. The feminist movement has indeed made great strides in calling attention to the scourge of wife abuse. It has pointed out the complicity of judges, police, and legislators in failing to recognize the gravity of the problem and failure to adopt proper legislation or even to implement existing laws. There has been a loud clamor for more responsible behavior by all involved in dealing with wife battering to recognize it for what it is, a criminal assault against a human being, and not a family squabble to be managed by civil court, family court, or referred for mediation. All these efforts are laudatory, but there is only one catch: this will not solve the problem of wife abuse!

There is general agreement that the justice system needs a major overhaul, but it is questionable when and if that will ever occur and even if it does, its efficacy remains to be seen. What we do know at this point in time is that the system has been a dismal failure and cannot be relied on to protect our lives and property. For example, eight consecutive administrations have conducted a "War On Drugs," with increasingly severe penalties for drug trafficking and with much more effective surveillance at points of entry to prevent the smuggling of drugs into the country. With billions of dollars spent and the army at the disposal of the government, the drug industry is thriving as never before. Parents who naively think their child is safe from this deadly epidemic because signs around the school have been posted declaring it a "Drug Free Zone" are likely to be bitterly disillusioned.

There is one key word, one crucial word that is at the core of the wife abuse issue, and that word is *dignity.* No, italicizing it is not enough. DIGNITY, **D-I-G-N-I-T-Y**. That is the beginning and end of it all. If women will be properly esteemed, then there will be no wife abuse. If this does not come about, all other efforts will be futile.

The reason I stress this so greatly is that we must focus our attention and efforts on what will restore the dignity of women, and we should not be taken in by any spurious methods, regardless of how logical they may seem and even what other salutary effects they may have. I hardly need to point out that obtaining the right to smoke in public was a hollow triumph for women. The ads may declare "You've come a long way, baby!" but puffing on a cigarette did not go a long way to elevate the dignity of a woman, and in fact did not even advance her cause by a single millimeter.

Let us not confuse power with dignity. There are dictators, tyrants who have absolute dominion and have the life and death of the population in their hands, but who may be totally lacking in dignity, and, even if they are feared, are not esteemed by anyone.

One of my patients was a woman who graduated college *Summa Cum Laude* and was the recipient of the Phi Beta Kappa Award, the highest award given for scholastic achievement. She graduated medical school with honors and became a board certified specialist. Her husband was a lazy lout who lay on the couch reading books while she was the wage earner, as well as the manager of an efficient home for their three children. She held a prominent position as medical director of a major health facility, with many subordinates. Her husband, who contributed nothing to the family, repeatedly berated her as being inefficient, and she swallowed it all. While he may not have physically abused her, he almost succeeded in destroying her, because in her desperation she made a serious suicide attempt. Here was a woman of superior intelligence, occupying an important position of authority, providing for the family, and totally lacking in self-esteem. This particular story has a happy ending. She was treated for her depression, received the proper therapy, got rid of her no-account husband, and reared her three children who love and respect her. Today she is a woman with self-esteem and dignity, and she credits her therapist for helping her achieve the strength to turn her life around.

There is no question that in a social system which is male dominated and in which women are disenfranchised in one way or another, the dignity of women may be seriously compromised. Yet, if we keep the single focus in mind, that the pivotal point is not necessarily power nor authority but **dignity**, we may be able to at least establish a valid theoretical foundation on which to build. Otherwise, it is conceivable that we may have a woman as President of the United States and a woman as Chief Justice of the Supreme Court, and a woman as Chairman of the Board of General Motors, and still have a rampant problem of wife abuse.

Chapter 9

What The Torah Says About Wife Abuse (II)

There are systems and disciplines that are based on certain axioms, certain givens, without which the entire system cannot exist. For example, the entire system of Euclidean geometry is based on the axiom that two parallel lines will never intersect. If you postulate that two parallel lines can intersect at some point, you have done away with the entire body of knowledge of Euclidean geometry. For someone to say, "I accept all the conclusions and principles of Euclidean geometry, but I do believe that it is possible for parallel lines to intersect," is utterly meaningless and is an intolerable, internal contradiction.

Fundamental to discussion of any Torah attitude is the Torah concept of life itself. If the latter is not accepted, then nothing in Torah has any relevance. This is stated clearly in the Talmud which teaches that all of the 613 mitzvos prescribed in the Torah are ultimately based upon the single principle, "The righteous person lives by his faith" (*Makkos* 24A).

The underlying principle of life in Torah is that everything –the universe, the world, mankind–was created for the sole purpose of bringing glory and honor to G-d. It is not coincidental that the first of the seven *berachos* (blessings) recited at the Jewish wedding ceremony and during the week of festivity following the wedding, is "Blessed be G-d who has created everything for His glory." From super galaxies to the egg of a mite, everything in creation was brought into being for the single purpose of bringing glory and honor to G-d. If one accepts this principle, then we can proceed with the rest of Torah. If one does not accept this fundamental axiom, then nothing one does is compatible with Torah, even if one were to be in technical compliance with the *mitzvos*. For example, if one were to observe *mitzvos* because one recognizes them as fair and just, as protectors of human life, and as constituting an ideal social contract, rather than because they were divinely ordained, one is not observing Torah, but rather following the dictates of one's own mind.

This basic tenet is variously expressed, and is the intended message of the *shema* which is recited daily: *kabbalas ol malchus shomaim*, acceptance upon oneself of the yoke of divine sovereignty. For there to be Torah observance, everything in life must be directed for the greater honor of G-d.

The derivative of this is that in Torah life there is no room for considerations such as "What is it that *I* want?" as motivation for any thought or action. The motivation must be, "What is it that *G-d* wants?" This is again emphasized in *Ethics of the Fathers*, "Negate your will before His" (2:4). It is no small feat to essentially eliminate the ego, but if one wishes to live a Torah-true life, it cannot be otherwise. Moses said, "I stand between G-d and you" (at Sinai, *Deuteronomy* 5:5), upon which the Maggid of Mezeritch commented, "It is the 'I', the ego, which stands as the barrier between G-d and you."

The Torah is well-aware of the human needs for companionship, for sexual gratification, and for perpetuating oneself via one's offspring. Yet all of these must be subordinated to the fundamental and comprehensive principle, and in regard to marriage, the Talmud says that the proper motivation for marriage is because that is what G-d wishes (*Sotah* 12A).

It should be immediately obvious that if one were to set aside one's own ego drives—for sexual gratification, for power, for acclaim, for pleasure—there would be no potential whatever for wife abuse, no seedling from which this ugly behavior could sprout. We have no choice but to come to the obvious conclusion: Anyone who abuses his wife is one who is derelict in the fundamental underpinnings of Torah, regardless of how meticulous he may be in his religious practices.

The will of G-d is that there is to be a marriage and a family, and that the latter is to advance the glory of G-d. The family is a team, if you will, whose ultimate purpose is, as is that of every individual, to bring honor to the name of G-d. If roles are assigned to members of the team in order for the team to be able to fulfill its function, it is totally irrelevant whether an individual receives the role he or she might prefer. Imagine a baseball team that is playing the deciding game in the World Series, and the only available catcher on the team says that he does not wish to be their catcher, and will only play if he gets to play second base!

Society has its ways of giving values to people and their roles, and it should be quite evident that contemporary society's standards are quite sick. A person who is a performer in the entertainment field and whose performance may even be of questionable morality, may earn millions of dollars a year, whereas school teachers, to whom we entrust the education and essentially the future of our children, may have to resort to the picket line to get a decent living wage.

How often have you heard the expression, "I'm only a housewife?" On the other hand, how often have you heard, "I'm only a lawyer," or "I'm only president of the company?" Who has established these values? On what basis are these evaluations of peoples' worth and importance made?

Remember, the key words are dignity and esteem. Incidentally, the Latin root of the word "esteem" is from the word meaning "to appraise." Society is "esteeming" people according to widely accepted but highly questionable standards.

Torah expects the union of husband and wife to be *kedushin* (holy), a process of holiness. While humans understandably seek various types of personal gratification, the marriage unit is to be of a different character. Its ultimate goal as *kedushin* should imbue anything and everything that goes on within it with the spirit of holiness.

The primary role of a husband, a wife, of every person, married or unmarried, is thus identical: To do the Divine will in this world and to bring honor to His name. How this is done may vary with each individual, but this is the function of the individual, and being the servant of Almighty G-d, commanded to do whatever mission He has intended for a person should be more than enough to give a person a sense of value, of self-worth, and dignity. If society wishes to attach a dollar figure, an academic degree, or a political position to dignity, that is its prerogative. We have already seen the moral paucity of society's evaluations. The true "esteem" of a person is related to fulfilling the goal for which one was created.

In Judaism there is the priestly tribe of the Levites, one branch of which are Kohanim. The latter were assigned special duties, especially in the Sanctuary, and they have privileges which non-Kohanim do not have. Torah requires us to recognize their special status as those chosen to conduct the service in the Sanctuary and other ritual functions.

I am not a Kohane, and I lack the special rights and privileges. However, I do not feel one iota less dignified than a Kohane. He was given one assignment and I was given another. I may feel badly when I do not do that which *I* am supposed to do, but it has never bothered me that I cannot do what a Kohane is supposed to do.

Each person, man or woman, is obligated to fulfill the purpose of their being. *That which gives value to the life of a man is precisely that which gives value to the life of a woman or a child*, and this value is not affected by nor contributed to by secondary attributes. Whether a woman comes to a proper conclusion that she achieves this goal by being a housewife, a professional, or an executive, should not have the slightest effect on her dignity, not on how she esteems herself, and not on how others esteem her. If she indeed fulfills her primary role, she is on an equal par with her husband, regardless of what he does, who he is, and how much he makes. A husband who thinks his wife to be in any way inferior to him for whatever reason is thus lacking in Torah conviction.

Do I really believe that these philosophical concepts will stop wife abuse? No, it is only when men will make the changes in themselves and take responsibility for their actions that abuse will stop. Yet, I am addressing those who picked up this book because, as Jews, they are concerned about this terrible problem among us. I do have a deep conviction that within every Jew there is a *neshama,* a divine soul which is pure and holy. The fact that some Jews may engage in behavior which is not becoming to them is due to the fact that every person has a potential for doing either good or bad, and a human being has freedom of choice.

I am not lecturing to the wife batterer, and I am not trying to get him to change his ways by teaching him Torah philosophy. I am speaking to Jewish men and women, especially to young men and young women who are **not** perpetrators or victims of abuse, and what I am saying to them is that every person has a *potential* of being involved either actively or passively in abuse, and that if we wish to prevent abuse, we must develop an orientation that will make abusive behavior impossible to commit and intolerable to accept. In particular, the community must develop an attitude that wife abuse is abhorrent, an atrocity which will not be condoned.

I am also speaking to those who are in a position to influence peoples' perspectives on life: i.e. rabbis and educators, to make their number one priority the instilling of the concept of the dignity of every man, woman, and child, in whomever they have the opportunity to teach. I am also appealing to those who counsel people involved in abuse to approach the problem with an attitude markedly different from that which now prevails among law officials and many counselors. I am asking them to realize that the dignity of a human being dare not be compromised, and that anyone who looks upon any human being as a second grade citizen is aiding and abetting the crime of wife abuse.

The Talmud states that on Judgement Day we will be asked, "Did you relate to G-d with reverence?" "Did you relate to people with reverence?" These two are placed on an equal footing. **There is no exception if the other person is one's spouse.** Abuse can be eradicated if and only if we will achieve the requisite reverence the Torah demands. This is achievable, but we must make the effort to achieve these principles, particularly since they are in sharp contrast with the toxic concepts that prevail in our environment.

Chapter 10

What The Torah Says About Spouse Abuse (III)

Earlier I quoted the Talmudic requirement that a husband should "love his wife as much as he does himself and should respect her even more than he respects himself" (*Yevamos* 62B), and I pointed out that anyone obeying this rule could not possibly commit either physical or emotional abuse. There are a number of other statements by Torah authorities compliance with which would rule out the possibility of abuse.

The 13th century Talmudist, Ravad, in the introduction to his work *Baalei Hanefesh* states that inasmuch as Eve was fashioned out of Adam, a husband must consider his wife an integral part of himself, and care for her and protect her as he would any other part of his body. We are reminded of the Jerusalem Talmud observation that if a person were to feel pain because his left hand was injured, he would hardly strike it with his right hand to avenge the pain it caused him (*Nedarim* 9:3). Similarly, even if a husband were to be angered by his wife, to act out against her is as though he were acting out against himself. Torah law also forbids a person to inflict injury against himself. A person who injures himself or strikes out against another person indicates thereby that he has no respect for himself as well as for others.

The Talmud recognizes the emotional sensitivity of a woman, and Maharal states that particularly because the husband is the dominant person in the home, he must be extremely wary of his wife's sensitivities *(Nesivos Olam, Ahavas Rea* 2). Rav states that a husband should be most cautious not to annoy his wife, because a woman is emotionally sensitive and is easily moved to tears (*Bava Metzia* 59). Rambam (*Ishus* 15:19) states that a husband must speak gently to his wife, and should neither be tense nor short-tempered. One of the Talmudic sages, when asked by his disciples to what merit he attributed his longevity, responded "I never said a cross word in my home" (*Megilla* 28A). Another stated a man should be most meticulous in giving proper respect to his wife, because the blessing of the household is by virtue of the wife" (*Bava Metzia* 59a).

While love is the bonding force in marriage, the Torah's concept of love is much different than that which prevails in the secular world, where love is frequently essentially self-love. Two people who are "in love" have found that the other gratifies one's needs, and whether these are sexual or security needs, they are essentially self-interest. The Talmud refers to true love as unconditional love, and states that love that is dependent on any factor may disappear when that factor is no longer present. Little wonder that western civilization is plagued with failure of the majority of marriages, which were based on evanescent cementing substance.

A marriage based on Torah has its strength in the ultimate goal of raising a family that will follow the Divine teachings. Beauty, charm, intelligence, security, all these have their place, and while their importance in a relationship is not denied, they are not of primary importance, and the relationship does not wither if the vicissitudes of life alter some of these secondary considerations.

Are there such marriages in today's world? Of course there are. It is just that there are not enough of them, and the adoption by Jews of the prevailing environmental attitudes has led to the meteoric rise of divorces in the Jewish community. Traditionally, divorce in the Torah-observant community was a rarity, but unfortunately this traditional strength of the Jewish family has suffered, no doubt because the full quality of the Jewish marriage has faded. The increased mobility in today's society, with more frequent changes in residence, has also weakened traditional family ties and has undermined the support system. Some of the attitudinal changes that have contributed to the relative fragility of the Jewish home have also contributed to the increase of spouse abuse.

I do believe there are many healthy marriages, where the focus on the primary role of the family is still maintained. However, I can speak authentically of only one which I personally observed, that of my parents.

My parents' marriage was one of 52 years duration. There was never any question that my father was the "head" of the family, but the phrase, "Let's ask Ima" (mother) was one that I heard frequently. There was a mutual reverence, and the attitude of our respect for our parents was due not only to our commitment to the Scriptural command, and not only to the Talmudic statement that "reverence for parents is equivalent to reverence for G-d," but also reflected our parents' reverence for one another.

Were my parents in love? Very much so. Did they "fall" in love? Yes, after they were married.

You see, in the Chassidic culture in which they were raised, marriages were arranged by parents. My father and mother met for the first time *after* the marriage ceremony.

I asked my father, "What about the Talmudic requirement that a person should see the woman before he marries her?" My father smiled, "That requirement was satisfied. The evening before the wedding there was a festive gathering. The men assembled in one room and the women in another. Somebody pointed out Ima to me, but I really had no idea who he was pointing to."

The Torah states that when Eliezer brought Rivka to become Isaac's wife, "Isaac brought her home and he loved her" (*Genesis* 24:67). Their love developed after the marriage, a much different state of affairs than the passion which so often brings men and women together today.

I can tell you this much. My parents' early life was racked by poverty, deprivation, stress, and *tzoros*. Any relationship that had been primarily based on considerations of self interest would likely have been shattered by the constant frustrations and hardships they experienced. These enormous obstacles were weathered and they triumphed over them, and their relationship blossomed into true love, the unconditional love that Torah advocates because it was based on a common ultimate purpose.

I will cite only one incident that I believe indicates the quality of their feelings for each other. My father developed cancer of the pancreas, which had spread to the liver. He was very knowledgeable about medicine, and he knew that for this particular type of cancer, chemotherapy was of no value. He said to me, "If chemotherapy could prolong life, I would probably be obligated by halacha to suffer the many discomforts of treatment. But since it cannot prolong my life, simply to suffer for no reason at all is not a *mitzvah.*" I concurred with him that there was no point in chemotherapy. For whatever reason, the doctor told my mother that chemotherapy was of little value, and that at most it might extend his life for three months. "Three months!" my mother exclaimed. "Why, if it could prolong his life even one day it must be done." My mother then said to my father, "We did not survive all the *tzoros* in our marriage only to be separated prematurely, and every day I am without you is premature."

My father then said to me, "I'm sorry the doctor gave her such information, because not only will the chemotherapy not extend my life, it may even shorten it if the side effects are too severe. However, if I do not take it, then mother will be forever tormented by the thought, 'If only we had insisted on treatment, he might still have lived.' I don't want her to be tormented. I know that I am subjecting myself to misery, but it is not purposeless. It is for the purpose of sparing Mother any distress." Then he added, "There were many things I did for Mother's happiness, and now I am given one last chance to do yet another."

My parent's marriage was not an exception. There are many wholesome marriages with mutual esteem and devotion. I cited this simply as an example of what the ideal is. Incidentally, with all due respect to my grandparents, I cannot advocate marrying an unknown person, and I do not believe that the type of "acquaintance" my father was provided is really in the spirit of the Talmud. However, if this stands at one extreme, the basis for most modern marriages, which is essentially a mutual fulfilling of each other's needs, is at the other extreme.

I must digress here on the noxious effects of the prevalence of self-interest which is the prime motivation in most of what transpires in western civilization. When Nancy Reagan launched her "Just Say No To Drugs" campaign, some psychologists interviewed young people for their reaction. Some 12 and 13-year old youngsters responded with, "Why? What else is there?" This response enables me to understand why all the efforts to curb drug use have been futile.

There is universal agreement that law enforcement cannot eliminate the scourge of drugs, and that this can only come about by eliminating consumer demand. It should be evident that the latter is unlikely to occur if a significant segment of our youth has no aspirations other than to get the thrill of the effect of chemicals on the brain.

The attitude of youth is merely a spinoff of the hedonistic perspective on life that prevails in the adult population. While many adults may not seek the thrills of intoxication by either alcohol or drugs, the fact that the goal of life is to get as much fun and pleasure as one can, leaves many young people with the only option for immediate pleasure being sex and drugs. Young people will not be frightened away by the danger of sexually transmitted diseases nor by the harmful effects of drugs, even if both are lethal. There is ample evidence that scare techniques do not work. The only hope to curb the dreaded epidemic of drugs lies in our ability to provide an answer to young peoples' question, "What else is there?," an answer that will be meaningful and acceptable to them.

Such an answer cannot be provided by didactic teaching alone, whether at home or in school. Children are unlikely to do as parents *say*, and are much more likely to do as parents *do*. If the parental life is spiritual rather than hedonistic, other-directed rather than self-directed, there is hope that young people may emulate them. Spiritual and other directed: These are Torah values, and encapsulate the essence of Judaism. Both drug addiction and wife abuse, among many other noxious behaviors, are incompatible with a spiritual, other-directed orientation toward life.

Let us recapitulate. While many social changes need to be implemented, the ultimate eradication of spouse abuse will occur when there is a mutual esteem, reverence, and true love, that will make abuse an impossibility. By the same token, society as a whole, and, for our particular purposes, the Jewish community must emphatically say "No more!" and indicate in every way possible that spouse abuse will not be condoned.

Chapter 11

What The Torah Says About Wife Abuse (IV)

This chapter would be better entitled "What The Torah Does **NOT** Say About Wife Abuse." Some husbands have seized upon the phrase "a kosher (decent) woman is one who complies with her husband's will."

Yes, this statement is indeed cited in the Midrash, and we will turn to its source in a moment. Let us first realize that it clearly has limitations. If a husband were to tell his wife to cook something for him on Shabbos, she would certainly not be permitted to do so. Doing the will of a husband may not be used to violate any Torah commandment, nor may it be used to violate any Torah ethic. We have already pointed out numerous references to the high standards provided by Torah for respecting one's wife and that the husband is cautioned to assiduously avoid upsetting or irritating her. The statement of "doing the will of the husband" may not be used as a way to violate the Torah requirement for respect of the wife.

The principle "The ways of Torah are pleasant" (*Proverbs* 3:17) is applied in the Talmud to halacha (*Sukka* 32A; *Yevamos* 15A), to rule out practices which would be incompatible with this principle. Tyranny in the household is abominable, and there is no way the Torah would condone this. Anyone using this Midrashic statement (praising the woman who abides by her husband's will) to oppress his wife is distorting Torah, not complying with it.

But let us look at the context where this statement appears. It is in the *Midrash* of Judges, c. 5, which relates the heroism of Jael, the wife of Hever, who saved Israel in a crucial battle by killing the enemy general, Sisera. Scripture tells how she lured Sisera into her tent, gave him milk to drink which caused him to become drowsy, and when he fell asleep, she drove a stake from her tent into his head. It is upon this episode that the Midrash comments that Jael was a decent woman who did the bidding of her husband, and the Midrash goes on to praise her, who by her heroism surpassed even the matriarchs, Sarah, Rivka, Rachel, and Leah. What is the relevance of this statement to Jael?

The commentary *Meam Loez* states that Jael's husband, Hever, had a peace agreement with Sisera. If so, then Jael's action was a clear defiance of her husband's will rather than a compliance!

Jael's heroism consisted of taking the necessary action to save Israel, even though she could have chosen to remain neutral because of her husband's pact with Sisera. She could have remained within her tent and minded her own business. Indeed, Radak interprets the verse in *The Song Of Triumph* of the prophetess Deborah, "Jael is more blessed than the women in their tents" (*Judges* 5:24) as commending Jael for her assertiveness and venturing out of her tent to attract Sisera and destroy him.

Jael understood that Hever's pact with Sisera was nullified by Sisera when he aggressed against Israel, and that the will of her husband was really that she should destroy Sisera if she had the opportunity. It was for this reason and in this context that Jael was praised for understanding what Hever would have wanted.

As an aside, the sages of the Talmud point out that even when Jael killed Sisera, she did so with the stake of her tent rather than with a weapon, so as not to transgress the scriptural prohibition against women bearing arms (unless in self-defense, *Deuteronomy*, 22:8). In other words, even when she took aggressive action, Jael did not compromise her femininity.

At any rate, the phrase "A kosher woman is one who abides by her husband's will" is not to be distorted to support tyranny. Such

distortion constitutes Torah abuse as well as wife abuse. Exploiting
this phrase to justify physical, sexual, or emotional abuse is a gross
violation of Torah.

Chapter 12

What Torah Says About Spouse Abuse (V)

The first four chapters on this subject should suffice to clarify the Torah perspective. However, I find it necessary to reiterate and expand on this theme in view of some books that have been written on the Jewish marriage that purport to present a Torah perspective, but which I feel are totally off the mark.

In *Path Of The Just*, Luzzatto warns that attempts at being pious and saintly can be treacherous, and that a person may think he is performing a mitzvah while he is in fact violating the Torah (c. 20). We must therefore exercise great caution in establishing standards of ethics and propriety.

One thing stands out blatantly in Torah. **THERE CAN BE NO COMPROMISE ON HUMAN DIGNITY.** There are countless references to this principle in the Talmud and ethical works. To cite just a few: "Maintaining the dignity of a person is so great that it may override halacha" (*Berachos* 19B); "Thus said G-d to Israel: 'Am I lacking anything that I must ask it of you? All I ask is that you love one another and respect one another'" (*Tana d'be Eliahu* 28); "Let the dignity of the student be as dear to you as your own" (*Avos D'Rabbi Nosson* 27:4); "One dare not demean any human being in the world" (*Zohar, Vayetze* 164A). The list could be continued ad infinitum.

Indeed, the Torah requires that in those instances when a person must be punished for a crime, his dignity must nevertheless be preserved (*Sanhedrin* 10A,B). Even if a person is executed for a capital offense, human dignity is not waived (*Deuteronomy* 21:22-23, Rashi). To assert that a wife may be treated with anything less than dignity is essentially considering her a non-person. This is anathema, and as far removed from a Torah perspective as one can be.

There are those who invoke the principle of *shalom bayis* to justify a wife's resigning herself to abuse. This reminds me of the visitor to Soviet Russia who was told that the Soviets had already achieved the millennium, and was shown that a lion and a lamb were living harmoniously in the same cage. "Amazing," he said, "How is that possible?" "Simple" the guide said, "Twice a day we give him a fresh lamb."

Yes, a wife may preserve peace in the household by silently accepting the control, nay, the tyranny of a power-crazed husband. This is hardly what the Torah wants. The Torah condemns human sacrifice. The Talmud cites the verse in *Jeremiah* (19:5) "I did not command it and I did not wish it," to refer to the daughter of Jephtha (*Judges* 11:30-40), and to the near-sacrifice of Isaac" (*Taanis* 4A). The latter was meant to test the devotion of Abraham, but was not permitted to go on to actual sacrifice. To say that the Torah advocates a woman sacrificing herself to tolerate lifelong abuse is unconscionable.

Shalom bayis is indeed a sacred concept, but it is the responsibility of *both* husband and wife to see that this is achieved. It is a mistake to think that the entire responsibility for *shalom bayis* rests on the shoulders of the wife.

One of the double standards that exists in Western civilization and is particularly intense in the Jewish community involves the attitude toward a failed marriage. As a rule, a divorced male goes on with his professional and business life, and if he is successful in these, he does not perceive his divorce as devastating. The wife, on the other hand, is more likely to react much more intensely to a divorce, believing that she has somehow failed her husband and children, and has not measured up to the ideal "woman of valor." *Shalom bayis* is a truly peaceful home, where harmony prevails.

Peaceful co-existence, particularly at the price of self-effacement by the wife is not *shalom bayis.*

It is true that the Talmud allocates the highest praise for a person who keeps his silence and does not return an insult. But this refers to a verbal assault by another person from whom one can walk away and one need not maintain an ongoing relationship with him. In such circumstances it is best to avoid a confrontation and conflagration. It is totally different when one is in an ongoing relationship, and the most intimate of all relationships, that of husband and wife. This relationship cannot be a master-slave relationship in either direction, and neither a husband nor a wife should be emotionally abused and have their dignity shattered.

There are yet other considerations. I believe we have established in previous chapters, with adequate Talmudic references, that the Torah requires a husband to respect his wife, and that he may not torment her. A community that essentially compels a wife to accept physical or emotional abuse in silence is being an accessory and accomplice to her husband's transgressions. Accepting abuse is not a virtue, else Solomon would have included it in the praises of "the woman of valor" (*Proverbs* 31). Each Friday night we sing the praises of the virtuous woman, among which we say that "her husband and children sing her praises." Nowhere does Solomon refer to resigning herself to abuse as being a virtue, and a society that demands such self-effacement and does not provide a woman with the resources and abilities to defend her dignity is an accomplice to the abuser.

The Talmud states that when Rabbi Nehunia entered the house of study he would pray that he should not make a mistake in halacha and thereby give cause to his peers to mock him. Rabbi Nehunia was not concerned that he might be humiliated, but rather that he would be the cause of his comrades sinning by mocking him (*Berachos*

28B). *If the lack of community services and cultural support deprives a woman of the ability to maintain her dignity, then the community is tacitly encouraging the abusive behavior and is an accomplice to the sin.*

The need to wield power and to be in control of another person is a serious character defect. To cultivate and perpetuate this trait is not doing a person a favor. It is quite like being kind to an alcoholic by buying him more liquor or to the narcotic addict by giving him money to buy heroin. It is a misguided kindness, and when the community condones abuse, it is not doing the abuser a favor.

In *Life's Too Short* (St. Martin's Press 1995), I pointed out that the need to dominate another person is invariably the result of a low self-esteem. A person who has feelings of unworthiness and inadequacy may try to compensate for them by lording over others to give himself a feeling of importance. A controlling husband must stop his domineering behavior; he must make the salutary changes in his character that will give him true self-esteem, rather than victimizing his wife.

It has been adequately documented that a husband or wife that is abusive to the spouse is likely to be abusive to the children as well. This is as true of emotional abuse as physical battering. Abusive behavior in the home is a crime against the spouse and a crime against the children. Furthermore, children reared in a home where there is abuse are likely to become victims of abusers or abusers in their own marriages.

It is interesting that children may have greater resentment against the "healthy" parent than against the abuser. Many children of alcoholics have said, "I wasn't that angry at my father. He was a sick person. But I can't forgive my mother for allowing us kids to be victims of his condition."

At the first sign of abuse, a wife should say to the husband, "Dear, I married you because I loved you and I want to continue loving you. I cannot love someone who does not respect me and who is abusive to me. I will cooperate in every way and work with you, with counseling if necessary, so that you have no need to act this way. However, my dignity is not negotiable, and I wish you to respect me as I respect you." If the husband is recalcitrant and continues to be emotionally abusive, the wife should seek counseling from someone with expertise in abuse.

The harmful consequences of emotional abuse are every bit as grave as those of physical battering. The one major difference is that physical battering requires immediate separation. **Allowing the woman to be exposed to a batterer while attempts at correcting his problem are being made is placing her life at risk**.

It is not unusual for a husband and wife to disagree on some things, and even to disagree sharply and loudly. While regrettable, such shouting matches do not necessarily constitute abuse. It is also possible that a husband may come home after a difficult day at the office where whatever could possibly go wrong went wrong, and he is in a very irritable mood. By the same token, it is possible that the children were in a devilish mood, and that by the time the husband comes home from work, the wife is both exhausted and irritable. Under such circumstances, foolish remarks can be made, which are soon retracted with an apology. Such isolated incidences may not constitute serious abuse. However, controlling the other person's actions and making demeaning and degrading comments does constitute emotional and verbal abuse and has no place in a marriage.

Some types of emotional abuse are: (1) name calling; i.e., stupid, idiot, jerk. (2) Sabotaging things the wife does so that she should appear to be inept. (3) Berating the woman as being an inadequate wife and mother. (4) Berating the wife's family. (5)

Making threats. (6) Undermining the wife's efforts to go to work or advance herself. Anything which impinges on the dignity of another person is considered abuse, and is a violation of Torah ethics.

Chapter 13

What The Torah Says About Abuse (VI):
Sexual Violence

In recent years, the issue of "marital rape" has been discussed in both the legislatures and the courts. As in so many other areas, Torah law has been hundreds if not thousands of years in advance of secular law.

That there was even any consideration whether or not forced sex is considered an assault is indicative of the demeaning secular attitude toward women. Torah law is explicit, as is stated by Rambam, the prime codifier of halacha: "He is not to have intercourse while drunk, nor in the midst of a quarrel; he is not to do so out of hate, nor may he take her by force with her in fear of him" (*Laws of Marital Status* 15:17). The *Tur* (Rabbi Jacob ben Asher), quoting his father, the halachist Rabbi Asher (*Rosh*), writes "Rape, even of one's wife, is forbidden." While in the latter part of the 20th century secular courts argued whether forced sex with one's wife is rape, the halacha defined it as such many centuries ago.

The halacha goes one step further. A woman is awarded the right to refuse her husband's request to have sexual intercourse in unusual ways. "If a woman claims that her husband does not lie with her in any way similar to the way husbands lie with their wives...this claim suffices for him to be compelled to divorce her" (*Tur, Even Ha'ezer* 154). Halacha upholds the woman's dignity.

The difference in attitudes toward forced sex is a consequence of the concept of sex per se.

Torah considers all human activities to be potentially spiritual, and the ethical writings expand upon the Scriptural statement "Know Him in all your ways" *(Proverbs* 3:6) to mean that everything a person does can be elevated to a spiritual level. If one understands the ultimate goal and purpose of life to be doing the Divine will, then keeping the body in optimum condition to enable one to do the divine will is also essentially a spiritual activity. Inasmuch as eating and sleeping and all other physiologic requirements are necessary for optimum health and function, they all become spiritual acts when performed with the ultimate goal in mind.

Appropriate gratification of the sexual drive is conducive to an optimal emotional state, and it too can be spiritual. This may well be the message of *mikva,* wherein purification prior to sexual relations indicates the Torah attitude toward sex. Inasmuch as the *mikva* is generally in preparation for sacred functions, its practice and preparation for marital relations is no exception. Forced sex is nothing but brute passion, and while being primarily an assault against the woman, it is also an abuse of the sexual act in itself. Forced sex is totally antithetical to a Torah way of life.

The secular attitude towards sex is apparent from the decadence to which sex has been subjected to in modern society. The social tolerance of perversions and pornography have degraded human sexual behavior far beneath that of brute beasts. In a culture that considers women to be sexual objects, it is not surprising that forced sex in marriage could be exempted from being an assault against a person.

Not only does Torah not require monastic abstinence, it does not even permit it. Sex is an important physiologic and psychologic component of human life, but like all other components, it should be performed at the level of human dignity, not at the level of animal passion, and certainly not beneath it.

Earlier we alluded to the phrase "A kosher woman is one who does the wishes of her husband." This is valid only when the wishes of the husband are compatible with Torah teachings. Sexual abuse is clearly antithetical to Torah, and instructors who prepare young women for marriage should make this clear to them.

Chapter 14

To Yeshiva Educators

In the previous chapters I suggested steps which women can take to minimize the likelihood of abuse. I pointed out that in the yeshiva world where marriage generally occurs at an early age, often when the young woman is 18 or 19, there is scant opportunity for such preparation.

We must divest ourselves of the delusion that in these marriages there is never any abuse. It is a fact of life that wife-battering does occur, and whatever the incidence is, it is unacceptable. Emotional abuse, defined as an attempt by the husband to control and dominate the wife is certainly not uncommon.

I know the young men who attend the yeshivas and the kollelim. They are fine young men, and there is no reason why any of them should become wife abusers. Some may not understand that their behavior is abusive, because they grew up with it in their homes, and they are actually unaware of the gravity of their behavior.

These are young men who have studied our great works of mussar, *Mesilas Yeshorim, Orchos Tzaddikim, Michtav M'Eliahu,* and various others. They have listened reverently as you have lectured to them on the importance of *midos.* The overwhelming majority of them become good husbands, but...

Yes, there are some who become abusers. I receive calls from abused wives, and many of the mental health professionals receive similar calls. Unfortunately, in most cases, by the time a woman calls for help, the abuse has been going on for years, and everyone has suffered greatly. In some of these cases it has progressed to the point where the marriage cannot be salvaged.

In the yeshiva world there are understandable efforts to preserve the atmosphere that prevailed in the citadels of Torah in pre-World War II Europe. It should be obvious, however, that the environment in which young men grew up in those days was radically different from the toxic environment that prevails in western civilization today.

We have done everything feasible to protect our young men from the noxious influences of the world, but we would be deceiving ourselves to believe that we have achieved anything near a hermetic seal. The external influences are antithetical to Torah, and although we can resist them in the form of avoiding *treifa* food, by observance of Shabbos, and by avoiding intermarriage, there are more subtle influences that are not immediately recognized as being in opposition to Torah *hashkofos,* and these can have a negative impact on marriage and family life. Neither male chauvinism nor modern feminism is compatible with Torah. While halacha assigns different obligations and rules to men and women, nowhere is there anything that justifies tyrannizing women, or equalizing men and women in every single aspect.

We have been taught proper midos by our *gedolim,* to whom we were exposed in the yeshiva and in their leadership of the community. We observed their every action, how they talked with people, how they were sensitive to people's needs, how they showed respect to everyone, including their students. Every gesture of a *godol* was a lesson in behavior.

However, there was one extremely important area where our exposure to them was limited. Except for rare occasions, we were not in their homes, and when we were there it was unusual for the rebetzin to be present. In most situations the rebetzin would prepare something for visitors and then leave the room. We were thus deprived of being able to learn from our greatest teachers how they related to their wives.

Everyone has a favorite story about the Chofetz Chaim, about Reb Chaim Ozer, about the Rebbe of Gur, and all our great luminaries. But alas, we did not have the privilege of learning by observation how they related to their wives.

But there were exceptions. Some people who were regular household members of our *gedolim* were able to report about what they observed, and the children of the *gedolim* could relate how their parents behaved toward one another. Our *gedolim* were as observant of the Talmudic requirement to give more *kovod* to one's wife than one does to oneself as they were of every other Torah ordinance. In the Talmud Rabbi Zeira said, "I never said a cross word in my home," and those who were privileged to see the home life of our *gedolim* saw these principles put into action.

Book learning is very valuable, but just as one cannot implement halacha without *shimush,* so are the teachings of *midos* only exercises in abstract thinking until we see them applied. Everything the *sifrei mussar* said about *anivus* took on new meaning when we saw how Reb Moshe and Reb Yaakov related to their students or to lay people who were not scholarly, their attitude and respect and their attention to these people's needs, and then we understood what the *sforim* meant by *anivus.*

What was true of previous generations remains true today. Your students learn what you teach them, but even more what you *show* them. They note how you put on your tefillin, how you wash your hands for *hamotzi,* and every other move you make, and they emulate you. But they have no access to your home life, and whatever they read in the *sforim* may remain abstractions.

There are some factors in the lives of young couples that can raise the level of tension in the home and thus raise the potential for development of abusive behavior. Many young men who continue as full-time Torah students after their marriage have financial concerns. Some receive parental support, some receive a stipend, some have an income from the wife's earnings, but in spite of the fact that they value their dedication to Torah study, they are unable to escape thinking about the future. How long will a father-in-law continue his support? (Even when support is forthcoming, a father-in-law may use it as a lever to control the young couple. If a dutiful daughter sides with her father, this may cause the husband to turn against her). How reliable is the *kollel* stipend, given the frequent financial crises? The wife's ability to work is compromised by her childbearing and care of young children. What happens when money is scarce? What does the future hold? If there is not a family business to absorb a young man, and if he is not pursing a profession, what then? Is *chinuch* the only option? If so, heaven knows that teachers are grossly underpaid, and what if someone feels unsuited to be a teacher?

Thoughts such as these can torment a young man, and may impinge on his ego. After all, the husband is supposed to be the provider. "Will I be able to fulfill this role?" Even if the wife is not demanding of extravagance, is it right to deprive her of some of the niceties of life that other women have?

A young man who feels his ego threatened may act out in a desperate attempt to bolster his sagging ego by "showing who's boss," and he may draw upon various Talmudic phrases which can be misinterpreted to justify his behavior. This does not necessarily lead to physical violence, but he may try to exert his authority by controlling what his wife does, and whom she talks to, and he may make demands which may be unrealistic, such as "When I come home I expect supper on the table, or else!" even though she may have three children in diapers to care for.

Young men need to be prepared for marriage, and I feel that the yeshiva has a responsibility to do so. Firstly, they are away from home, so that their parents cannot help, and furthermore, they may accept the authority of the yeshiva more readily. Such preparation should begin years before they consider marriage.

To compensate for the lack of firsthand observation on how a Torah-true person should behave toward his wife, I feel that the yeshivas must emphasize the proper *midos* as they apply to marriage. The numerous sources in the Talmud which discuss the dignity of the woman and how a husband is expected to respect her should be *repeatedly* cited and explained, and the distortion of Talmudic passages which are misinterpreted to justify tyranny in the home must be corrected. Young men must come to know that this is not a trifling subject, but something of the highest importance.

The works of Torah have a power unequaled by anything else in the world. Just think of how many times we have read the story of Joseph and his brothers, yet every year when we read how Joseph wept when he saw Benjamin, our hearts ache along with him, and when we hear how he revealed his identity to his brothers and said "*Ani Yosef,*" we feel chills running up our spine. Similarly, who is not moved to tears when we read how Rabbi Akiva returned home with 24,000 disciples, and when his wife Rachel greeted him and his students tried to keep her away, Rabbi Akiva rebuked them saying, "All that I know and all that you know we owe to her." Regardless of how many times we read this episode, we are emotionally moved.

The Talmud says that the world would have been desolate of Torah had Rabbi Akiva not taught Rabbi Meir, Rabbi Yehuda, Rabbi Yosi, Rabbi Shimon, and Rabbi Elazar. It was Rabbi Akiva's disciples who gave Torah to the world. Let us then remember his words, and every time we are electrified by Reb Chaim's analysis of a difficult Rambam, or by a brilliant essay of the *K'tzos,* let us remember that everything we know of Torah we owe to Rachel, the wife of Rabbi Akiva. Let the young men whose wives take care of the children and make a home for them, often while also holding a job, let them know that Rabbi Akiva cherished and appreciated Rachel, and that when he bought her a golden crown, he said, "She suffered along with me in my acquisition of Torah."

The accounts of how our great Torah personalities honored their wives is every bit as important as the intricate discussions of halacha, but this must be emphasized and students must be taught to know that their success in life depends on their giving proper honor to their wives *(Bava Metzia* 59A).

The Jewish home, the Jewish family–they are the secret of our survival. This hallowed institution must be founded on the mutual trust and respect between husband and wife. This issue is nothing less than one of *pikuach nefesh* which demands the undivided attention of all Torah authorities and educators.

Chapter 15

Preparation for Marriage, Or How To Deal With Abuse

What a terrible title for a chapter! How can one be so cynical, so pessimistic, and have so negative an outlook as to anticipate that every marriage may result in abuse?

Look, when you were a baby, your mother took you to the doctor to have you immunized against tetanus (lockjaw). During your first year of life, you had three injections, each of which was painful, and each of which was followed by 48 hours of fever and misery. Some loving mother you had to have done that to you! Yet, if you are or will be a loving mother, you must do that for your children. Why? Because tetanus is a terrible disease, and once you get it, there is little that can be done to treat it, therefore the only thing to do is prevent it at any cost.

The fact is that **the chances of your ending up with a physically or emotionally abusive husband are greater than your stepping on a rusty nail at sometime in your life.** You hope that neither will happen to you, but you must take precautions, just in case.

We do many things to protect ourselves against what we hope will never happen, immunization being just one of them. We pay for fire insurance, flood insurance, theft insurance, accident insurance, disability insurance, and heaven knows what else. These may be costly premiums, but we cannot afford to be unprepared for what we hope will never happen. Why single out marriage as the only matter for which one should be unprepared in case things do not work out the way we like? Again, the chances of having an abusive husband are greater than the chances of having your house burn down.

Some women have described their battering husbands as being dual personalities: loving people who have a crazy component to them. They say, "That's why I stayed with him. There is so much about him that I love, but then this monster part emerges. If I could only find a way to keep that monster part locked up, he'd be the best husband any woman could ask for." That description does not fit all abusers by any means, but it does fit some.

For this latter type of person, it is possible that the abusive part might never emerge. This may be the kind of guy who would not become abusive unless he has a victim. No victim, no abuse. In such cases, adequate preparation against abuse may actually avert the abuse.

I am *NOT* blaming the wife for bringing out the worst in the abuser. It is just like having a well-guarded house, or the "club" on your steering wheel, because the presence of an adequate defensive system is a deterrent which discourages a would-be burglar from trying. If the man you are dating is someone who has the need to control, to tyrannize, or to dominate, and you are someone who does not let yourself be controlled, tyrannized, or dominated, he will leave you and find another more suitable for his needs. If you should marry someone who has an abusive potential and you are not a person who can be easily abused, that potential may never manifest itself. In any case, whether or not you can discourage abusive behavior, you should be prepared to cope effectively in the event it should occur.

No matter what philosophic views one might have, the facts of life are that a person cannot exist without the means to obtain the necessities in life, and that means **having money**. If a woman lacks the capacity to support herself, and is totally dependent on her husband for support, she has given him a powerful instrument for control. If the husband has no need to control and dominate, this economic dependence never becomes an issue, and there are many happy marriages where the husband is the sole provider and the only one with earning capabilities. In such cases, the husband and wife have their roles in the family, there is mutual love and admiration, and each respects and values the other's contribution. But where this is not the case, and the husband has the need to control, and the wife has no way to be economically self-sufficient, the grounds are fertile for development of abuse. Just how a woman would be self-sufficient is not of major importance, but some marketable skills are: secretary, nurse, financial advisor, social worker, court stenographer, lawyer, teacher, automobile mechanic if you will– just something that one can fall back on if necessary. *Young women would be well advised to prepare themselves with a capability of earning. Even if all goes well, there is often a need for two wage earners in the family, and when the children are at the age that they can care for themselves, the woman can be gainfully employed.*

Secondly, the motivation for marriage should not be seeking self-fulfillment via a relationship. Let me clarify that.

It is of interest that from a Torah perspective, the *mitzvah* of procreation is incumbent only on males. Although she is encouraged to marry, a woman may elect to remain unmarried. Torah law is psychologically sound, and the fact that a man is required to marry and have children but that a woman is permitted to choose otherwise indicates that it is possible for a woman to feel fulfilled even without marriage, whereas this is not true for a man. There are many mitzvos which are incumbent upon a woman, and from the Torah perspective, she can have fulfillment in these.

A woman may decide that she wishes to have a family and be a wife and mother, and this is certainly her right to choose. Raising children and contributing to the wholesomeness of a family is indeed a noble and most worthwhile cause, and a woman who does this has every reason to have a sense of self-worth. The problem arises when a woman feels bereft of self-worth and needs a relationship to vindicate her. She is then *dependent* on the praise of her husband, to acknowledge her, and to tell her how much he loves her and admires her. As with economic dependence, this can become a tool of domination in a husband who has a need for control.

It is certainly pleasant to hear the sweet words, "I love you," and I only wish that husbands and wives would continue to use these enchanting words in their marriage just as they did during their courtship. To enjoy them is one thing, but to become dependent upon them is another.

You may not like the analogy I am about to give, but I think it is valid. As an authority on alcoholism, I am often asked, what determines alcoholism? We are not talking about the drunkard who staggers from bar to bar, but the question is often posed, "I enjoy a glass of wine before dinner, and I may even have it every day. Does that make me an alcoholic?" My answer is that if one can eat without the glass of wine but does enjoy it when he has it, that is not alcoholism. If, however, one cannot eat *unless* one has had wine first, then one is an alcoholic even though the quantity consumed is not great. Why? Because one has become **dependent** on alcohol, and it is the *dependence* that leads to the addiction.

I believe that the same is true of the woman who needs herself validated. A woman may certainly enjoy being needed by her husband. The question is, is she dependent on his validation for her sense of self-worth? If so, she is at the risk of being a candidate of abuse. Why? Because her husband has something which she desperately needs, and if he is the controlling type, he may exploit her neediness for his own purposes.

One of the ironies of such a situation is that the more the woman is abused, the lower her self-esteem becomes, and the **more** dependent she becomes on the abuser to validate her. This is why an abused wife may try to appease and placate the husband in every way possible, in the hope that he will validate her, which of course, he does not do, and this results in a vicious cycle of abuse and progressively deteriorating self-esteem.

Take a good look at yourself. Do you have a feeling of self-worth without someone telling you so? Are you dependent on what others think of you for your self-esteem? If so, begin to look for ways in which to bolster your sense of self-esteem so that you will not be dependent on others to validate you, not even on your husband. You can then enjoy the relationship in a much more relaxed manner. There are many fine books on self-esteem development, and achieving a more positive sense of self can enhance happiness in many ways, in addition to improving the quality of a relationship.

Any number of women have said they had some misgivings about their future husbands, but were rushed or pressured into consenting to the marriage. A lifetime relationship should not begin with such doubts, and when such misgivings occur, the young woman should avail herself of an empathic and competent advisor who can help her investigate these feelings and come to a well-thought out decision.

Any number of abused women say that they would have left the marriage, but they had a terrible fear of being alone. There is no question that being alone is unpleasant, and indeed the Torah states that Adam was given a mate because "It is not good for man to be alone" (*Genesis* 2:18), and this is true of woman as well. The Talmud also states, "A woman may be satisfied with any kind of husband rather than being alone" (*Yevamos* 118B, Rashi). However, this Talmudic statement is simply describing a state of mind, and is by no means to be misconstrued as a recommendation.

To the degree that a woman cannot tolerate being alone and is dependent on a man for companionship, to that degree she weakens herself in the relationship. Again, if the husband has no need to take advantage of this and is pleased to provide the woman with the companionship she craves, there is no problem. If, however, he recognizes her dependence (which is not at all a difficult feat) and takes advantage of it to dominate her, she is at his mercy and at risk of being abused.

It behooves a woman therefore, to strengthen herself so that being alone is not terrifying. She can then relate to a man without the feeling of dread of what would happen if he were to leave her or if she were to leave him. A woman should learn how to enjoy solitude, and develop interests which would allow her to enjoy life even in absence of a companion.

The pattern is evident. Anything which increases a dependency of the wife on the husband contributes to the possibility of abuse, *if* the husband has this potential. The less a woman feels dependent, the more equal she is in the relationship, and the less is the likelihood of her accepting abuse in silence.

Having become somewhat familiar with what comprises abuse–whether physical or emotional–let me suggest that if you have grown up in a home where there was abuse, whether spousal abuse or child abuse, you should avail yourself of competent therapy before entering into marriage. I have earlier alluded to the phenomenon of generational perpetuation of abuse; i.e., that a child who grows up in an abusive environment is at risk of becoming either an abuser or a victim of abuse. I know that the logic is just the other way around, that the daughter who witnessed her mother suffering at the hands of an abusive husband would steer away from any man that gave the slightest hint of having any abusive tendencies. But forget the logic. The facts are otherwise, and if you are a child of an abusive parent, you are at greater risk of becoming involved in an abusive relationship. Get yourself into therapy with someone who has expertise in treatment of abuse problems, so that you can interrupt this generational perpetuation.

Get to know your emotions and what to do with them. At the risk of oversimplification and overgeneralization, I would like to point out an interesting gender-related phenomenon. Many men are unable to tolerate a feeling of hurt, perhaps because they believe it is not masculine to feel hurt–men should be made of tougher material. Their psychological system therefore converts "hurt" into "anger." It is not unusual for a man who has experienced something which, by logic, should have caused him to cry, to instead go into a rage.

With women it is often just the reverse. A woman may feel it is not feminine to be angry, and her system then converts "anger" into "hurt". An experience which, by logic, should have provoked an angry response, instead results in her crying. The problem with this is that feeling hurt may contribute to feeling powerless, and we have noted that feeling powerless increases the susceptibility to abuse.

The solution to this is to get to know your feelings. Men have every right to feel hurt, and women have every right to feel angry. Anger need not result in screaming or breaking things, and there are ways of managing anger so that it does not become rage. There are also ways of dealing with anger so that it does not result in harboring grudges and long-term resentments, and I have dealt with this theme at some length in *Lights Along The Way* (Mesorah, 1995). Proper management of anger need not result in either unconscious repression nor destructive rage, and it need not be converted into hurt, self-pity and feelings of powerlessness.

All the recommendations I have made could stand on their own merits; i.e., they are of value over and above being a deterrent to abuse. Economic self-sufficiency, a self-esteem that is not dependent upon the opinions of others, the capability of feeling content and secure even in the absence of a relationship, and the knowledge of and management of one's emotions, all these are features that strengthen one's personality and are of intrinsic value. Hence, even if there were no concerns of vulnerability for abuse, these are extremely worthwhile traits and abilities to have, and I suggest to parents that they encourage their daughters to acquire them.

I anticipate being asked what can be done in the Yeshiva/Chassidic culture where the practice is for young women to become engaged at 17 or 18 and marry soon thereafter, where many of these couples have very brief contact prior to marriage, often with only several dates prior to engagement and usually none afterward. How is a young woman of 17, who is just about ready to complete high school, to acquire the deterrents to abuse that I am recommending? Are there any recommendations for these young women to help them avoid abusive relationships?

Let me first state that the system is based on two premises, neither of which is foolproof. The first is that in the *shidduch* process, the young woman's parents will investigate the character of a prospective son-in-law and his family background. The defect in this is that some of the warning signs of abuse potential may not have been evident in the yeshiva environment, and unless one has access to the most intimate and reliable contact about the young man's family, it is difficult to know the truth about the home life. Even in highly reputable families there may be tyrannical domination by the husband, which the son then assumes to be normal, and which he is likely to emulate in his marriage.

The second premise is that a young man who is a yeshiva student and a Torah scholar will not be abusive because Torah observance precludes abuse. As I have pointed out earlier, there is no immunity, and abuse does occur even among observant men. The frequency with which this happens is unknown, particularly because Jewish families are very secretive about what goes on at home. Even if the incidence is less than in the general population, the problem does exist and there is no guarantee that a yeshiva student will not be abusive.

It would therefore be wise for all young women to prepare themselves adequately for marriage as mentioned earlier, but I do not see the feasibility of this in this segment of the Jewish community. Several years ago, one of the leading rabbis, alarmed by the rise in divorce rate in the observant community, suggested that there be several additional dates before an engagement is announced. His recommendation was rejected, but it is doubtful that several more dates would enable the average 18-year old woman to be able to sufficiently evaluate a young man to detect any signs of abusiveness.

In the absence of the opportunity to take preventative measures, one must fall back on early identification of a problem. To these women who marry very young and who become mothers I say, be on the alert for attempts by your husband to control you. Do not believe that the role assigned by the Torah to the husband gives him license to control, to tyrannize, and to belittle. You have a right to be treated with dignity and respect, and you do not have to tolerate either physical or emotional abuse. If your husband is in any way abusive to you, I suggest you promptly contact a competent counselor who can work with you and your parents to strengthen you and provide a support system. You will then have the opportunity to think about what you can do to put an end to the abuse, how to call this behavior to your husband's attention and make him realize that you will not tolerate abuse, and thus enable him to take the necessary steps to eliminate such behavior.

The goal of recognizing the abuse early is not to cause the breakup of a marriage. To the contrary, it is to enable a marriage to grow and thrive. Accepting and tolerating abuse results in bitterness in the home and has a deleterious effect on both the parents and children. Some young men may not even be aware that their behavior is abusive, and they may have a mistaken notion that the role of the husband is not only as titular head of the family, but also a dictatorial one. For many, this is how they were raised, and it is simply their learned behavior. They need to be corrected, and the earlier this is done, the more viable, durable, and wholesome a marriage will be.

Chapter 16

When Alcohol Is Involved

The two strong traditions about Jewish husbands is that they do not beat their wives and that they do not drink. If the woman who finds that her husband is an exception to the first of these is in trouble, how much more so if she discovers that he is both a batterer *and* a drinker. This is real *tzoros,* right? Not necessarily. Oddly enough, the reverse may be true. Although the track record for treatment of batterers is less than a great success, there is actually more hope if the battering occurs *only* as a consequence of alcohol intoxication.   Some batterers have been violent with or without alcohol, and the prognosis in these instances is not good. However, if the battering *never* occurs in absence of alcohol, there is some grounds for optimism.

The reason for this is that many alcoholics do recover, and a successful recovery eventually results in the emergence of a radically different personality. It is similar to what the Rambam writes about a person who has done sincere *teshuva:* "I am a different person, and I am not the same person who did those things" (*Laws of Teshuva* 2:4). It would be wonderful if the same could be said for the non-alcoholic abuser, but regrettably clinical experience does not support this.   I have had personal experience in treating alcoholics for the past 35 years, and I have had abundant contact with others in the treatment field, and we have indeed found that where there is a good recovery from alcoholism, the abuse that was incident to alcohol does not recur, unless, of course, there is relapse to drinking.

Abstinence from alcohol is not the same as recovery. While avoiding alcohol is an all-important first step in recovery, it is only that: a beginning. If nothing about the person changes other than that he no longer drinks, this is not considered recovery. In the trade we use the term "dry drunk" to describe this situation. The person is indeed "dry," but in every other way is the same drunk he was. There is no essential change in character, and there may be relatively little change in behavior.

I can claim a degree of authority in regard to alcoholics, inasmuch as I have treated over 30,000 alcoholics in my career. I have fairly intimate knowledge about the behavior of people who have achieved quality sobriety. There is simply no resemblance between the sober person and the person who drank.

The recovering alcoholic must undergo major characterologic changes, among which are the attainment of honesty, humility, forgiveness, and spirituality. He must work on eliminating character defects, and in fact may achieve a finer development of character than some people who never drank at all. I have not found these changes forthcoming unless the alcoholic has accepted and practices the 12 step program of Alcoholics Anonymous. The changes in character may be very gradual, and it may take a long time to overcome character defects and undergo changes in thought, feeling, and behavior, but these do occur in true recovery. It is equally important that the spouse of the alcoholic participate in the 12 step program of Al-Anon family groups.

Alcoholics Anonymous had its origin in the Oxford Group, which was a Christian group. The Christian flavor has remained in the format of the meetings, in that they generally close with the Lord's Prayer. The predominance of meetings being held in church social halls and basements (because few synagogue doors were open to them) has also conveyed a religious tone to the program. Consequently, people who are concerned that there may be a missionary or evangelistic element to Alcoholics Anonymous have been reluctant to participate in this program.

I have tried to set things straight in my book *Self-Improvement? I'm Jewish!* (Mesorah, 1995), wherein I point out that the content of the 12 step program is very, very Jewish, and may even have had its origin in Jewish ethics. Unless some isolated individual tries to exert a missionary role in AA, there is, to the best of my knowledge, no danger of proselytizing.

Alcoholism is a life-long disease which can be successfully arrested. We do not refer to an alcoholic as being "cured," because that would imply that he is now like every other "normal" person and can drink safely or socially. This is not true. Attempts to return to controlled drinking have invariably resulted in relapse to alcoholic drinking. Relapse is a particularly high risk during the first year of recovery.

If battering has occurred *only* incidental to alcohol intoxication, and the husband has entered a recovery program, there is reason for optimism that the battering will not recur after sobriety is achieved and stabilized. This does not mean that the wife should promptly reunite with the husband after he has "dried out" or even after he has completed a course in rehabilitation. Rather, the wife should be guided by a family counselor and utilize the experience of other women like herself, whom she may meet in Al-Anon. After the husband has been sober for perhaps a year, and if he continues active involvement in Alcoholics Anonymous and if his therapist recommends that it is time to reconcile, then the latter can be done. Premature reconciliation, before both spouses have had sufficient time to work their respective programs, is fraught with the danger of relapse to both drinking and battering.

What is true of alcohol may often be true where abuse has occurred *only* in relation to use of other mind-altering chemicals. Here again, promises are of no value whatever, and consideration of reuniting can be only after there has been extensive 12 step program involvement, with the concurrence of the therapist that it is time to reunite.

I cannot stress sufficiently that abstinence from alcohol does not in itself constitute recovery. One young executive refused to accept that he had a problem with alcohol, in spite of his wife's many entreaties, and even though his erratic behavior was pointed out to him. One morning he awoke to find the furniture in shambles and the interior of the house appearing as though a tornado had swept through it. His wife and children were not there, and when he found them to be at his in-laws, he went there, asking what had happened.

"You don't remember anything?" the wife asked. The husband, who had an alcohol-induced amnesia, could not recall anything, and refused to believe his wife's description of his violent behavior when he came home drunk the night before. It was only when their 11-year old daughter tearfully confirmed the wife's story and cried "I was afraid you were going to kill Mommy," that the husband accepted her account. He then promised that he would never touch another drop, and said that he would promptly get a crew to repair the damage in the house and would replace the broken furniture.

"That is all fine," the wife said, "But I am not moving back with you until you receive treatment for your drinking problem."

"Do you think I am crazy, that I will ever drink again after this?" the husband said. "I never had any idea what alcohol could do to me. Now that I have seen it, you can be sure I will never take another drink until the day I die."

The wife remained firm. "I know you feel that way, but drinking is not something you can control without treatment. Unless you go for help, I'm not moving back."

The husband protested that he could not take time off from the office to enter a treatment center, and furthermore, his reputation in the community would be permanently ruined if it were discovered that he entered a treatment center.

The man went to his minister and wept with remorse, pleading for him to intervene on his behalf. The minister called the wife and impressed upon her how sincere her husband was, and that he was completely shattered because of what happened, and that she could certainly rely on his promise not to drink again. He told her how important it was for the children to have an intact two-parent home. In short, he convinced her to return.

The man made good on his promise, and did not drink for four whole weeks, following which he reasoned that if he could abstain for four weeks, he was not an alcoholic. He was soon back into his destructive drinking pattern.

In both battering and drinking, remorse and sincere promises mean nothing. At least with alcoholism, entrance into a comprehensive treatment program, which will address both the alcoholism and the abusive behavior, holds out some hope that once stable sobriety is established, the abuse may not recur. While there obviously can be no guarantees, my experience has been that the characterological changes that the alcoholic undergoes during his recovery are also effective in eliminating abusive behavior.

Chapter 17

Beverly's Story

"I'm writing this not only with the thought of helping others, but also because I think it will be helpful for myself. Many times I've tried to put things out of my mind because they are so painful, but I think at times it is necessary to think about them. These things that happened to me are, after all, part of my life and will always be. I don't think one can make believe they never happened.

"All I wish to tell you about myself is that I was molested as a child and that left me with a very deep feeling of insecurity. I did not come from a religious background, but did become observant as an adolescent.

"I was introduced to my husband by a friend. Looking back, I can see that there were warning signs. He used to make insulting remarks to me and laugh at them. This hurt me, but I thought this was his way of being cute and that he didn't mean what he said. Sometimes when he helped me on with my coat he was very rough. But when you're starved for security and for someone to love you, you are blind to such things.

"After the marriage he was very rude to me, and this wasn't even in a joking way. I went to see a rabbi, who told me that I didn't have to put up with this and to get a divorce. Then he asked me if I was pregnant, and I said I was, and he said, 'Then it's too late.'

"At the beginning he was mostly emotionally abusive, except for two times when he threw things at me. We continued to have several children. At first when I complained to him, he would promise to change, but then he began saying, 'It's too late for me to change. This is the way I am. Take it or leave it.' Where could I go with five children? So I took it. For the sake of keeping peace in the house I put up with everything, trying my best to please him.

"My husband got in with some bad people and did some things which got him in trouble with the law. He ran away to Mexico, and while he was away I got on welfare and received some help from the community. That year was a very peaceful one, and then he told me he was coming back because things had been straightened out with the legal problem. I went to my rabbi and told him that I had a year of peace for myself and the children and that I didn't want to take my husband back, but he said, 'You don't kick a horse when he's down,' and said he would talk with my husband and get him to change his ways.

"My husband came back and right away went back to his previous behavior. I told the rabbi and he said, 'What can I do? He doesn't listen to me. Just try to appease him even if he doesn't treat you right, and eventually he will change.' But the more I tried to do everything he wanted, the worse he became.

"Then he started getting physically violent with me and with the children. Once I ran to call the police and he ripped the phone off the wall. My oldest daughter ran to a neighbor and called the police, who came but did nothing. They told me to get a court order of protection, but the rabbi said I shouldn't and that he would take care of my husband, which he didn't.

"I kept on living in this terrible situation because I didn't have anywhere to go. Meanwhile, my oldest son was reaching the age when he would need a *shidduch* and I knew that if I took any action it would ruin his chances. After my first three children were married, I finally decided I couldn't take it anymore. Even though I might be hurting my younger children's chances for a *shidduch*, I felt I was at the breaking point.

"I heard on the radio about a woman's shelter and I made an appointment. The people there were wonderful. I entered a support group, and they gave me courage and strength. I was able to stand up to my husband and tell him that if he touched me I would put him in jail forever. He sees the difference in me and has stopped pushing me around. There is no love between us, but the house is quiet.

"I still have two children at home. They don't like when I stand up to him because he screams and acts crazy. I told them that if I don't stand up to him he will think he can get away with it. They don't realize that if I let him abuse me he will abuse them as well. I can see where all my children are mixed up. In some ways they love their father and in some ways they hate him.

"I know I did not do my children a favor by bringing them into the world in such a marriage. I should have left him at the beginning. I would have had one child to raise, which I could have done well and might have remarried to a kinder person. Now I have five children, all of whom are mixed up, and I know they are having problems.

"From my experience I would like to tell women who are abused not to accept promises that he will change and not to take advice from people, even from rabbis, who don't understand the problems of abuse. When you first feel abused call a women's shelter and ask to talk to a counselor. Get into a support group and begin building your own strength. Maybe you will leave your husband and maybe you won't. But if you do stay, it will not be with the false hope that he will change for the better."

Chapter 18

Emotional Abuse: Marcia's Story

When the term wife abuse is used, one most often has the image of a battered wife, a woman physically injured by a husband who is physically stronger than she. However, abuse can occur without any physical contact whatever. A woman can be beaten and crushed emotionally as well as physically, and the consequences of emotional abuse can be every bit as devastating.

In some ways, emotional abuse may be even worse than physical battering. The degree of social insensitivity to battered wives notwithstanding, it is at least possible for people to recognize physical bruises and broken bones. With all of the shortcomings of the legal system, there is nevertheless some avenue of appeal for protection, and in some cities there are shelters for the battered wife who needs a place of refuge. In absence of physical battering, emotional abuse may arouse little sympathy. So what if she doesn't like the way he talks to her? Big deal! Emotionally abused women may not even find a sympathetic listening ear.

What is emotional abuse? Let Marcia tell her story.

"I was 22 when I met David. I had just completed training as a cosmetician. People said I was attractive, and I had been quite popular.

"My parents were rather simple people. My father ran a small print shop, where my mother worked as well. There was my younger brother and I. I believe I had a good childhood. We were people of modest means, but I never felt I was ever deprived of anything, nor did I ever aspire to much. I was very much Daddy's girl, and felt loved by my parents.

"Religion was not a big thing with us. My brother was Bar Mitzvahed, but I was not Bas Mitzvahed, and it really never bothered me. Our home was kosher out of respect to my mother's parents who visited us and we wanted them to feel welcome, but when we ate out we didn't care. My parents belonged to a conservative temple, we attended services on the holidays and on other occasions when friends celebrated Bar and Bas Mitsvahs.

"I met David at my girlfriend's wedding. He was a friend of the bridegroom. He was tall, handsome, 28, and had just graduated dental school. It was love at first sight. He swept me off my feet and I was on cloud nine. We dated frequently, and my parents were thrilled with David. Their fondest dreams had come true. I would marry a dentist and be financially secure for life.

"Were there any warning signs of what was to come? Very few, if any, and if there had been two dozen obvious ones it would not have made any difference. I was enchanted, the luckiest girl in the world.

"David's father was a prominent businessman, who was well-known in the Jewish community. He was involved in all Jewish communal activities. David was very proud of his father, and often talked about him and his achievements. I did not sense at this time that by glorifying his father he was putting my father down. After all, how could the proprietor of a small print shop compare with 'Mr. who's who' of the community? I did not pick up at that time that David was condescending. He was going to rescue me from the depths of ignominy to become a reputable person in the community. He was going to be my savior, but I didn't know this then.

"David had his ideas. He did not want his wife to work. There would not be an economic need for that. His father would equip his dental office, and his income would be more than adequate. Besides, David was an only child and he felt he had been deprived of brothers and sisters. He wanted to have a 'whole bunch of kids,' and expected to start our family right off, which would make steady work unrealistic. It sounded good. Why not? I loved children.

"David said he was more religious than I was, and we were to have a kosher home, which was fine with me, but we were also not to eat out, because there were no kosher restaurants in our town. I was to prepare all the meals, always. This was no problem for me either. What I did not realize then was that by setting himself up as more religious, David became the authority in religious practices, which of course I had to follow, and only he knew what was permissible and what wasn't. Again, I could not see at that time that this was one of his ways of trying to control me.

"My father could not afford the kind of wedding that David's family wanted, but they said not to worry. They were people of means and David was their only child, and he was going to be married in style. Little did I think in those star-studded days that I would one day hear, 'You were a nothing. I picked you up out of the gutter. You are what I made you.'

"I did get pregnant within a few months and had a difficult pregnancy. My morning sickness lasted throughout the day, and I could not tolerate cooking. David was upset that dinner was not on the table when he came home, but there was just no way I could do it. I suggested that we eat at our parents' home until I felt better, and David did so very grudgingly, letting me know that I was being derelict as a wife.

"Our first child was a boy, and Evan was a colicky baby. Nights were difficult, and David would not get up with the baby. He needed his sleep because of the delicate nature of his work at the office. The baby's crying annoyed him and he said I must be doing something wrong that the baby cried so often. I didn't know what it was that I was doing wrong, because I was following the pediatrician's advice, but obviously I must have been doing something wrong. Sometimes when the baby's crying disturbed his sleep, he would pull the pillow over his head and say, 'What kind of mother are you anyway?'

"Evan outgrew his colic, but David did not outgrow his irritability. Needless to say, he never changed the baby's diaper. That was beneath the dignity of a professional person, and if on occasion my caring for Evan resulted in dinner being a bit underdone or overdone, he berated me for my clumsiness. I took all his criticisms in good faith.

"David knew it all, and I knew nothing. On occasions when we met with friends, he would later tell me that I should just listen to the conversation and not say anything because I did not understand anything about either politics or business, and he was ashamed of my stupid remarks. I had no reason to assume he was wrong, so I just shut up.

"Slowly David began detaching me from my friends. They were improper influences on me because we were more religious and they did not observe what we did. Then we began to eat out at non-kosher restaurants, and David said he must do the ordering because I wouldn't know what is and what is not permissible at a non-kosher restaurant. This did seem logical at the time, and I had no awareness that David was just extending his control over me. I can see now that each time he gained another bit of control, he became hungry for more, very much like a conqueror who extends the boundaries of his country, with his goal being world domination.

"I gradually began to feel stifled, but what was I to do? My parents still thought I had lucked out by marrying David. They never heard how he insulted and belittled me, because he was always a gentleman in their presence. We did have a beautiful home, much more than I had dreamt of. Yet I was crying myself to sleep every night.

"Our daughter was born just a little more than a year after Evan, and David, who wanted to have many children, began resenting the children because I was giving more attention to them than to him. 'No wonder some men philander. You women drive them to it.'

"During our sixth year of marriage David's father died of a sudden heart attack. Being the only child, David felt it was his obligation to look after his mother. He would go there first thing in the morning, and after work have supper with her, returning home quite late. I hardly had a husband anymore. But what was I to do? Complain that he cared for his mother? Other husbands came home late after getting drunk at the bar. I should be thankful that my husband was late because he looked after his mother.

"I should have been thankful, but I wasn't. I loved David very much, and I wanted him with me. I loved him in spite of his deflating me. He wanted to be worshipped, and I was desperate enough to agree to worship him, and to absorb all the put downs and be his loyal servant. As miserable as I was, being there alone with the children so often, I did not think I was being abused.

"One night, when Debbie was about five, she ran a high fever, and I called David at his mother's to come take her to the emergency room, only to have his mother tell me that David had stopped off briefly after work and had left for a meeting. I got Debbie to the hospital in a cab. She was diagnosed as having a common virus and sent home. David came home after eleven, and when he found that I had called at his mother's home, and I said that he had not told me anything about a meeting, he became very angry. 'I don't have to give you an accounting of my whereabouts,' and he stormed up to bed.

"Things went downhill from there. David later admitted he was seeing another woman, and when I pleaded for him to break that relationship, he agreed that he would do so eventually, but he could not break it abruptly because he had to consider her feelings. Her feelings? What about mine? I guess they never counted.

"I became a nervous wreck. I was anxious during the day and couldn't sleep at night. I got a prescription for valium, and I will admit I took too much of it. It was the only thing I could do to escape from my anguish. David said I had become a pill junkie. He was right. I had become dependent on valium, was getting forgetful and often dropping and breaking things. David said he didn't want to be married to an addict. I didn't know where to turn for help, and David did nothing to get me help.

"David and I grew apart, and after several futile attempts at marriage counseling we were divorced.

"After the divorce I got into treatment and was able to get off the valium. Incidentally, I don't blame my addiction on David. While he did cause me to feel miserable, I was the one who took the pills for relief.

"In therapy, which took over two years, I began to realize that I had let David put me down. I thought I had accepted his abuse because I loved him so much, but I discovered that it wasn't really love. You don't love someone who abuses you. It was my fear of being alone, and I had become so down on myself that I thought that I couldn't live without David. What I thought was love was really fear.

"I began to take my life in my own hands. I got a job in a cosmetics boutique, which was just up my line. I love my work, and customers come back and ask for me personally. I take an interest in them, and they appreciate it. David never appreciated anything I did.

"I'm certain that I'm not the only woman to whom something like this has occurred, and if I have any message to give to other young women, it is 'Don't accept the first putdown. A husband who truly loves you will never try to berate you. Suffering in silence only feeds a man's need to control.' Perhaps if I would have stood up to David right from the first, he would have had more respect for me."

Chapter 19

Malka's Story

Malka's story is presented essentially verbatim as she courageously presented it in a public forum. It is succinct and precise, and it also stresses several crucial points:

(1) There is concealment by people involved in *shidduchim* of significant facts in a person's past. This is a frank violation of the Scriptural command "Do not stand idly by while your neighbor's blood is being spilled" (*Leviticus* 19:16). Think a moment. How would you feel if you discovered that your daughter's husband had a severe emotional problem which was covered up, and she is now trying to care for three children and a mentally ill husband?

(2) While there may be subtle warning signs, a woman who is charmed by a man often ignores these.

(3) Early incidents of abuse are often set aside: "I still loved him."

(4) There is fear of leaving the marriage: No where to go, no way to manage, concern about public opinion.

(5) The man is a saint in the community while being a monster at home.

(6) Ignoring the abuse problem takes a deadly toll on everyone: the wife, the children, and even on the abuser himself.

(7) These problems can exist next door to you without your having the slightest suspicion.

Now let Malka tell her story.

"It doesn't happen in frum communities. Certainly not in ours. Oh, come on, there are hardly any incidents at all like the one you are describing. So what if a man loses his temper and hits his wife once in a while? My father had a temper. She must have done something to anger him." **For too long the abused woman has suffered in silence. So have her children. It is a problem that touches too many Jewish women and their children. The next woman could be your daughter, sister or friend.**

"He came highly recommended by a rebetzin of a well-known yeshiva who was acquainted with us both. He had *smicha* (ordination), was good looking, intelligent, a college graduate with a Master's Degree. His family was well known in their community. She never bothered to tell me he had substantial personality problems, that he had gone off the *derech* (straight path) for a good year or so, and that his relationship with his parents and siblings was problematic.

"I came from an Orthodox, Jewish home, had graduated from a frum girl's school, had been working for a number of years, and was attending college in the evenings. My relationship with my parents and siblings was quite a loving and caring one. I grew up with a somewhat critical mother and never realized the effect it was having on me. I was quiet, and kept to myself a lot.

"I was 'in love'. With him I felt I had found the missing part of me. I felt as though I had always known him. We spoke about his learning, the future family we would raise, the responsibilities of husband and wife. I was so happy! **I ignored the warning signals**. He once told me that he hated his mother and despised his father. I can still recall my feelings that I would 'give him the love his parents had obviously never given him and make him happy.' He was jealous of his siblings, but particularly of an older sister.

"My father did not like him. **Another warning signal I ignored.**

"It was not until we were married for a while that disturbing parts of his personality became glaringly visible. He lied to me, and put down my religiosity while not being terribly observant when it came to many laws. I accepted him for what he was and wasn't.

"We had our first child. Arguments became more frequent. He had a temper – something I had never seen while we were going out. He yelled, insulted me and my family. He threw breakable objects. We stayed with his parents for awhile and I saw an unhealthy family relationship. Still I stayed. **I never spoke to my parents about my problems**.

"I was still in love with him and now had a child. We moved out of town. By the time we had our second child he had threatened to break my arm, was making obscene phone calls to other women, had thrown many objects at me, some missing me by a hairsbreadth, and some finding their mark. Still I stayed. I felt caught in a trap. How would I manage without him, what would people say, how would my family feel? I never told anyone about my personal problems.

"I tried to get him to come with me to marriage counseling. He refused. He threatened to divorce me if I continued counseling. I stopped. Then I began to believe him that there was something wrong with me.

"He was making a great name for himself in the community. I began getting involved with the community, but never shared anything personal with anyone. He encouraged me to do things. I was often happy. The majority of the time he was very loving and we had fun together. The bad incidents were infrequent, so that in between I could forget about them, diminish their importance, and put them somewhere in the dark recesses of myself.

"He was becoming more and more critical of me and the children. He made nasty remarks about women, putting down the entire gender. He was constantly hurting the feelings of those around him. Somehow, it was always my fault. He was making a very good living. I received an 'allowance' for food. Anything else I wanted to purchase required permission.

"I went to counseling behind his back. I began to see that we both had problems that had to be worked on. I was afraid to approach him with it. When I did, upon the insistence of my counselor, he asked me if I was having an affair with the man and threatened to kill him if I continued seeing him. I foolishly stopped. He was in total control – just the way he wanted it.

"Over the subsequent years he became a compulsive gambler. It wasn't until he became a drug addict that things went from bad to worse. There were doctors who were constantly supplying him with various pain killers. Some of them realized that he was abusing them, but didn't stop giving them to him. Some were frum doctors. We were all abused verbally, the children stopped inviting friends over, we didn't have any company, and he started becoming physically abusive to me. I ended up in a shelter with my children when I became fearful for my life after a number of physical assaults on my person.

"We are divorced, but the effects of his actions live on. **Don't you recognize us? We are your neighbors.**"

Chapter 20

Ruth's Story

"My name is Ruth. That is to say, that's what my name is now. It used to be Catherine, and I took the name of another convert when I converted.

"I grew up in the home of an alcoholic father who beat and abused my mother. He used to beat us also when he got drunk, and when I turned 15 I had the guts to tell him that if he dared lay a finger on me I would kill him, and then he stopped. I couldn't stand it at home anymore and went to live with an aunt and uncle.

"My sister, who is six years older than me, is married to an abuser. My aunt used to tell me that the only way to be sure not to have an abusive husband is to marry a Jew. 'They don't hit, they don't drink, they don't gamble, and they don't run around with women.'

"I never had much concern about Jews one way or another. My father never had anything nice to say about anyone, and Jews were no exception. I didn't like them and I didn't hate them. But one thing I knew for certain was that I didn't want to go through the hell that my mother and sister were suffering.

"Any of the psychologists that tell you that daughters of an abuser seek someone like their father don't know what they're talking about. I didn't want anyone who was remotely like my father, and don't give me the business about unconscious. Even my unconscious didn't want anyone like him.

"When I went to college, I tried to date mostly Jewish guys. Sheldon was in law school, and we seemed to hit it off right from the start. His family were Reform Jews and they were nice people who didn't really care much that he was marrying a *shiksa*. Why should they? Sheldon's two sisters were more *shiksa* than I was. They couldn't tell you the difference between Chanukka and Rosh Hashanah. Sheldon's grandparents, though, were not thrilled about it, and for their sake, I converted.

"That's not quite true either. Even though I was brought up with hardly any religion, I felt that our children would have to have something to go by. My adolescence was in the 70's when there still was all of the craziness of the 60's going on. Maybe religion couldn't provide the whole answer, but at least it was something to hang on to. I went for instructions to a Reform rabbi's classes, and he was a real decent person. I liked what he said about Judaism, and when I finally converted it was more for myself than for Sheldon's grandparents.

"Now I have to tell you this because it's important. Sheldon said that he knew that I was brought up to celebrate Christmas, and that if I wanted a Christmas tree he would have no objection. I said I really didn't care all that much, but that when children came along I did not want a Christmas tree in the house because if we were going to raise the children Jewish I didn't want to confuse them.

"Sheldon and I lived together for almost a year, and we got married just after he graduated law school. Sheldon's father was a lawyer and wanted him to join his firm, but Sheldon said he wanted to make it on his own and not on his father's reputation, and he took a job as Public Defender. I worked as a secretary. We were going to delay starting our family until we were more financially secure.

"But I got pregnant during our first year of marriage. Sheldon was angry at me as though it were my fault, totally ignoring that he had something to do with it. Birth control pills are just not 100% perfect. He said he wanted me to have an abortion because we weren't ready for children, but I couldn't stand the thought. We were certainly not destitute and we could afford a child.

"I don't know what got into Sheldon, but that is when he seemed to change. I worked throughout my pregnancy, but he wanted my paycheck. That was strange to me, because I always deposited it in our joint account anyway. What difference did it make whether he or I deposited it?

"Sheldon seemed to adjust to the idea of the baby, and appeared to be happy when Stevie was born. However, he never helped care for Stevie, and would never get up for him at night. One time when I was down with a fever I asked Sheldon to help with the baby and his answer was, 'You wanted him, you take care of him.'

"Sheldon is a very bright man, and when he found out there was an opening at a corporation which was looking for a lawyer, he applied and got the job. They recognized they were going to have a very resourceful young man on their team.

"Stevie was born in November, and I did have a Christmas tree that year. Next year Sheldon said to me, "Don't forget, you can't have a Christmas tree this year. Stevie is old enough to notice things. I said, 'Of course. That's what I had said to begin with. It was you who wanted me to have one.' I can't tell you why, but there was something in his tone of voice that upset me.

"Sheldon began sulking. I asked him what was wrong, but he said never mind, it was nothing. I asked him if there were problems at work and he said no, but he continued to be very irritable. He would shout at me for no apparent reason. I thought maybe he was under too much pressure at work, but he denied this.

"I had not gone back to work after Stevie was born, and Sheldon was now on a decent salary, so that we really had no financial problems, but he began to be very tight with money. He wanted me to account for every cent I spent.

"When my sister's daughter had her First Communion, Sheldon refused to go with me, which was okay. I wanted to buy her a gift, a $100 savings bond. Sheldon refused, saying I would have to buy it out of my own money. I told him that I didn't have my own money, because I had deposited all my earnings in our joint account, but he said I had probably put away some money when I was working, which was not true. When I again asked him to please let me buy the bond, he slapped me across the face.

"The worst fear of my life had come true. But I refused to admit that Sheldon was an abuser. This was just a freak accident, it would never happen again, even though he made no attempt to apologize. But he just continued becoming bossier and nastier.

"This was totally out of character for Sheldon, and I felt that there must be something emotionally wrong. Maybe there was some stress he was under that he wasn't telling me about. His sexual interest had dropped off. I thought he should talk to a psychiatrist because he just wasn't himself, and when I suggested this to him I really meant it for him as well as for myself.

"'So now I'm crazy, am I? Well, if I'm going crazy it's because you're driving me there!' I asked him what I was doing wrong, but he just huffed and walked away. He did not hit me again, but he did throw things at me, and once narrowly missed my head with an ashtray. I don't have the kind of horror stories that you hear from some abused women with repeated beatings, broken bones, and being dragged around by their hair, but for me it was enough.

"I don't know why I had the guts to stand up to my father but not to Sheldon. Maybe because with my father I had somewhere to go. Then I could go to my aunt, and I didn't have many financial needs then. But now I had a baby and needed support. Besides, my aunt had her hands full with my uncle, who had suffered a stroke. I certainly couldn't go to my sister who was suffering from an abusive husband. I couldn't talk to Sheldon's parents, because they worshipped the ground he walked on. I did talk to the rabbi who converted me. He was sympathetic, but said he had no influence whatsoever with Sheldon, whom he had met only a few times.

"Sheldon's personality and behavior continued, and at one time, when he was in a calmer mood I said, 'I don't know what's happening with us, but we are drifting apart. That's not good for me, for you, or for Stevie. I would like us both to go to counseling and see if we can straighten things out.' Sheldon's response was that all of the marriage counselors he knew have messed-up lives themselves. Most of them are divorced, and if I have any dreams about getting a divorce, I should forget about it. He and his father have powerful connections in the court, and I would lose custody of Stevie and get very little in the way of a settlement.

"I still tried to fix things up, but the harder I tried, the worse it became. One day I watched a TV program about abuse and called the Shelter Hotline. Without Sheldon's knowledge I began going for counseling. I discovered that I was not at fault, and the counselor agreed with me that something emotional had happened to Sheldon, and that he was in some kind of a depression. He could be helped if he went for treatment, but that was out of the question. Through the shelter I saw a lawyer, and told him about Sheldon's remarks about his powerful court connections. He said not to worry, and that I was to gather data and document everything, and not let on what I was planning. We later decided to have a meeting with Sheldon. Since he would not go to the counselor, the counselor (plus a huge muscular man for protection) came to the house one evening. I told Sheldon that I had been in counseling for several months, and that I had hoped he would join me in getting the marriage back on track, and that we still had the chance of doing so, but if he did not choose to do this, all the pieces have been put in place for me and Stevie to move out and file papers for divorce, and that we had taken adequate precaution against any power play on his part.

"I actually felt sorry for Sheldon at this session because he reacted like a man who had been beaten. Thank G-d he did not put up a fuss. He agreed the marriage was over, that he would not fight for custody of Stevie. I moved out of the house and moved in with a wonderful woman who just loved Stevie and I was able to go back to work. Our divorce eventually went through, and I received a reasonable if not completely satisfactory settlement.

"To this very day I don't believe Sheldon was a typical abuser. Something inside of him had snapped, but he refused to deal with it. I still think my chances of getting a non-abusive husband are better with a Jewish man. I am now dating a Jewish man, and I have hopes of a good relationship. I don't relish being alone for the rest of my life. I am not fooling myself that my next Jewish husband is going to be a saint, but I still think my chances are better."

Chapter 21

Repetitive Themes

A number of women were asked if they would share their personal stories as abused wives. All responded with essentially the same opening lines: "It is hard for me to write about this, but if I can help even one woman avoid what I experienced and suffered, it will be well worth it. In retrospect, one of my biggest difficulties was being so alone. I didn't think there was anyone else like me. I thought that Jewish husbands were saints. If my husband was abusive, it must be my fault. I was doing something wrong that provoked him."

Other themes that recur are that the abuse often begins with the husband's demand for total control, of the finances, of the car, of friends..."I though I was lucky because he didn't drink or run around with other women"..."Everybody loved him. Outside of the house he is very likeable, and no one around believed what he was like in private life."

Some women say, "I can now see some of the warning signs that were there even before we were married. If he got frustrated he would kick the couch or hit the wall...he was jealous of me, and wanted to know where I was every minute of the day. What I thought was love was really his wanting to be in complete control of me."

A number of women said they became apprehensive about going through with the marriage, but the parents said, "You can't back out now. The invitations are out and several hundred people are coming," or, "It's just the normal premarital jitters," or, "You are an ideal couple. He's a good Jewish boy from a fine family, and you are a smart Jewish girl. Look at all the presents that have come in already. You'll see, things will work out beautifully and you'll be very happy." If they went home to their parents after a battering they would be told, "Go back and make the best of it. You don't break up the home. A lot of adjustments have to be made."

Husbands who beat their wives or chase them with knives would say, "Look what you made me do!" and the women believed it was indeed their fault. Beatings occurred during pregnancy, and some women were certain that they had suffered miscarriages due to the beatings.

Some women asked, "Does beating always begin when the wife is pregnant for the first time?" Invariably when the beatings began with the first pregnancy and the wife wanted to leave, she would be told by her parents or rabbi "You can't leave now. It's too late." Some said, "There was rarely any affection with sex, just a mechanical relationship."..."Isn't it true that a Jewish wife should never fight back?"

Without exception, the wives tried to shield the children from observing the batterings, and the beatings would often occur after the children were asleep. In many cases the husband was physically abusive to the children as well.

Many women were afraid to call the police because they did not wish to cause a scandal. Others report calling the police, who elicited a promise from the husband that he would behave. The husband's family often took his side, "Our son was never like that. You must be doing something to him to make him that way."

Most accounts describe attacks of intense, senseless rage, with brutal beatings, often provoked by some rather insignificant thing, such as buying something without first obtaining the husband's consent, or spending too much on an item, or the food not being to his liking. Some describe a "dual personality," with the battering personality being almost unrecognizable. "When he gets into his rage his eyes have a different look. I'm sure he could kill."

There is a classic book on sociopathic behavior, *The Mask of Sanity,* by Cleckley, where the author argues that sociopaths are actually psychotic, even though they do not appear to have any gross distortions of reality such as delusions or hallucinations. This psychosis does not respond to any known treatment.

In listening to or reading the accounts of abused women, one may get the feeling that battering husbands, like sociopaths, have some kind of psychosis even though they may not be delusional or hallucinatory. This conclusion should not be misconstrued as a defense of the batterer, that he is a sick person who deserves sympathy. The important conclusion we must derive is that at this point in time, initial attempts must be directed not at curing the batterer or preserving the marriage, but at protecting the abused wife. First efforts should be to keep the wife safe from further battering, and this invariably means separation. Once the wife's safety is assured, consideration can be give to therapy and counseling; the possibility of preserving the marriage can be considered calmly, without pressure, and with guidance from competent counselors.

Chapter 22

A Place Of Refuge And Beyond

The Scriptures are replete with divine commands to look after the needs of the oppressed and the persecuted. Indeed, the *Midrash* states that even when the persecutor is in the right and the persecuted is in the wrong, G-d still looks after the one who at that particular moment is in danger (*Vayikra Rabbah* 27:5). The Torah provides for cities of refuge for a person who killed someone accidentally, to protect him from relatives of the victim who might be seeking revenge (*Numbers* 35:10-28). There is a Torah obligation to provide refuge for someone who is fleeing from an assailant. It is therefore the responsibility of the Jewish community to see that a battered wife has recourse to a safe harbor and since she may have to take her children with her, there must be proper accommodations for them as well.

Ideally, the woman and her children should remain at home, and the offender, the batterer, should be the one to leave. Until the legal system provides for this, we must be concerned for the immediate welfare and indeed the very life of the woman who is at risk, and this means providing prompt access to shelter, available at any time, day or night, seven days a week. As a medical student, I was introduced to the emergency room service, where my instructor said, "When an accident victim is brought in, your very first concern is that there be an open airway. After you have established that the person is breathing, you can then proceed with other essential treatments. But unless you have made sure that he is breathing, all the intravenous and blood and other medications you may give him are worthless."

Much the same is true of a battered wife. First we must see that she remains alive and is not subjected to further beatings. This means, primarily, immediate access to appropriate shelter.

Assuming there is a shelter available, the woman may arrive with nothing other than the clothes on her back. There are many needs she will have, and these must be addressed promptly.

Every effort should be made to get an Order of Protection (see note, page 38) that would allow the woman to return to her home and to compel the batterer to leave. If this is not feasible, then she must be helped to find satisfactory accommodations, since in absence of these, she may be forced to return to the batterer, and this is out of the question.

While there are a number of social agencies that may provide help in various ways, these are often bogged down with bureaucratic red tape which the woman can ill afford. Most agencies operate five days a week, 9 am to 5 pm, and the woman who needs help in the middle of the night or on the weekend is out of luck. There may be emergency welfare funds available, but "emergency" may not mean same day availability. The woman may not have means of transportation to get to the various agencies. Furthermore, she may not have the necessary documents, such as birth certificates, to satisfy the agency, and finally, she may be told that her husband's income precludes her receiving welfare aid! Such is the consequence of the existing social system. The husband batters the wife, and she may not be able to secure the help because her assailant is making too much money! If she is eligible for welfare, it may still take some time until a check is actually in her hand. There is thus a need for discretionary funds that can be made available immediately.

A battered woman is certain to need legal counsel, but her husband is hardly likely to foot the bill. The community should have an attorney available promptly, one who is well versed in litigation of abuse cases.

An actual case history demonstrates my point. Irma fled from her husband who had threatened to kill her. She had no where to go and ran with the children to the nearest police station, 10 blocks away, in the middle of the night, and remained there until the morning when she went to a friend's home. She had no clothes for herself or the children, and called the police to accompany her to her home, which they said they were unable to do. She finally had two friends go with her, and fortunately her husband was asleep.

Irma called the local mental health service, who referred her to a local charitable agency. She needed an attorney to obtain an Order of Protection, but without funds to hire a lawyer, all that was available was a public defender. By the time she got to him it was late Friday afternoon and nothing could be done until Monday. (In some communities an Order of Protection can be obtained at any time, day or night).

Irma's friend was helpful, but it was evident that she could not remain at her home very long, since she simply could not accommodate three more people. Irma lived in a city with a small Jewish population, perhaps one-hundred families, and there was no formal Jewish social service available. She contacted the local rabbi who was at a loss what to do. She looked around for a place to stay, but all there was was the Salvation Army, which was only for men. The friend could not put Irma and the children out on the street, and she was able to stay with her for a little over a week, when the public defender was finally able to get an Order of Protection, which evicted the husband and allowed her to return home. Needless to say, the husband did not leave her the car.

Irma applied for welfare, and was told that her husband's income made her ineligible. No amount of explanation helped. The welfare worker had to abide by the rules. Until there was a divorce, she was ineligible for welfare.

Irma's parents lived in a distant city. She did not want to burden them with her problem, since her father was a heart patient. Their home was too small for Irma and her children anyway, and furthermore, going to live there would mean uprooting the children and taking them out of school mid-year, which was unfair to them.

Irma again contacted the rabbi, who tried to be helpful, but didn't have any money or housing at his disposal. The rabbi contacted the husband who said that everything would be fine if she had the Order of Protection rescinded. He promised he would not hit her again, but refused any treatment. Irma felt she had no choice, and returned home, living in constant dread that her husband would resume his abuse.

Three months later this indeed occurred. Irma ended up in the emergency room with multiple injuries. This time the rabbi contacted her father who came and took her and the children back with him. A coordinated system of help within the community would have avoided this outcome, which was far from the optimum for either Irma or the children.

While Irma's problem occurred in a small Jewish community which did not have a Jewish service agency, this scenario could well occur even in a larger Jewish community. Many communities have not come to terms with the reality of wife abuse.

In such communities, it is essential that some Jewish organization, perhaps the Jewish Family Service, should organize meetings with the community rabbis to provide information on wife abuse and professional training to enable rabbis to recognize the problem, to make the proper referrals, to know what resources are available, and to serve as a helpful participant in a team approach. Additional funds may be necessary for hiring staff, developing a shelter, and providing emergency support. Community representatives can visit other communities where services are already in place to see what the needs are and how they can be provided. Finally, ongoing community education is essential so that abused women can know that help is available and where to seek it.

Chapter 23

The Aguna Issue

Shalom bayis (peace in the home) is of prime importance in Judaism. Restoring peace in a home where *shalom bayis* has been lacking is a *mitzvah* of the highest order. There are many times when couples may not see eye-to-eye on everything and there may be disagreements which undermine the *shalom bayis*. There may be problems in communication which result in disharmony, and it is a great *mitzvah* to help a couple discover their errors in communication and thereby help them achieve a healthy and happy relationship.

Disagreement and communication problems are not abuse. These can be worked with, and it is situations such as these where efforts should be made to restore *shalom bayis* and avoid the dissolution of a viable marriage.

Abuse, however, is an entirely different situation. Overwhelming experience has confirmed again and again that as a rule, abusers do not change and their promises are empty and misleading.

In recent years, much attention has been called to the *aguna* problem, the "chained" woman who is trapped in a non-viable marriage. This results from the fact that *halacha* specifies that a marriage can be dissolved only by the death of a spouse or a *get* (halachic divorce document), and that the *get* must be given willingly by the husband. Contrary to civil divorce, no one can issue a divorce decree, not even a *beth din* (rabbinical court). The wife is essentially at the mercy of the husband, whose refusal to give her a *get* may cause her to be "chained" in the marriage. Unless a woman receives a *get* she may not remarry, and if she remarries without a *get*, children born to this second marriage are *momzerim* (illegitimate), a status which can never be removed and which they pass on to their children unto eternity. A *momzer* may not marry into a Jewish family. The *aguna* is thus in a very oppressive predicament.

Halachic authorities are seeking ways in which to free the *aguna* from this bondage, which for all practical purposes means convincing the husband to give a *get*. Theoretical considerations as to whether marriages can be made in a fashion that would make annulment a possibility, or signing pre-nuptial agreements that would compel the husband to give a *get* if the marriage proved to be non-viable have been given serious consideration, but have not met with the approval of many *halachic* authorities.

In some cases, the husband uses his power to refuse a *get* as a vehicle of extortion, to gain custody of the children or to extort huge sums of money. Rabbinical courts have often found themselves essentially helpless to aid the *aguna*. *Halacha* does not allow for dispensations or alteration of existing Torah law, and the rabbis must work within its framework.

Nuclear fission can be used constructively to provide unlimited sources of energy, to diagnose diseases, and to treat malignancies. However, if it falls into the wrong hands, it can be a devastating terrorist weapon. It should be understood that to Torah-observant people, Torah law is a fact of reality, as immutable as all laws of nature. Torah law is no more alterable than is the law of gravity. Just as scientists cannot prevent the constructive source of nuclear energy from being misused destructively by terrorists, there may be no way in which *halachic* authorities can prevent Torah law from being abused by a terrorist husband.

How true is the Talmudic statement that the Torah can be an elixir of life when applied properly, but in the hands of unscrupulous people, Torah can be misused as a deadly poison (*Yoma* 72b). The recalcitrant husband who refuses to give a *get* is converting life-giving Torah into a deadly weapon.

The Talmudical sages and the Torah authorities that followed them moved heaven and earth together to free an *aguna*. They were primarily concerned about a woman whose husband disappeared, and although it might be assumed that he is dead, as for example, missing in action during wartime, there is no firm evidence of his death. Torah authorities have gone to all lengths to accept sufficient shreds of evidence to be able to assume *halachically* that the husband did indeed die and that his wife is free to remarry. The modern problem of a woman being an *aguna* because of a recalcitrant husband's refusal to give a *get* was not a serious one in the days when the Jewish community was close-knit and interdependent, when rabbinical orders were obeyed, and when social pressures were adequate to convince a husband to give a *get*.

Today, things are much different. The social structure is much freer and rabbinical courts are essentially impotent. The *aguna* may be trapped in her situation for years.

A husband's refusal to provide a *get* is an obvious abuse of power. He has taken a provision of the Torah and made it into a weapon of tyranny and oppression. *Without exception, every case of aguna, every case of a husband's refusal to give a* get, *will reveal a history of a woman's having been abused during the marriage.* This last and perhaps greatest abuse of power, refusal to give a *get*, occurs only in individuals who were abusers and who had been either batterers or tyrannic controllers of their wives.

In virtually all of these cases, the abused wife had turned for help to her family or to rabbis earlier in the marriage, and they had made efforts to reconcile the couple, convincing her to return to the marriage for the sake of *shalom bayis. It is these cases that may result in the woman becoming an aguna.* The benign intentions of those who sought to preserve *shalom bayis* unfortunately contributed to the plight of the woman who became an *aguna*.

As we have noted, the abusive husband progressively increases his domination during the marriage, and the more the wife becomes helpless and dependent, the more this feeds into his craze for power and control. Parents and rabbis may think that they have preserved *shalom bayis* by advising the wife to return to an abusive husband on the basis of his promise to change, but they must realize that *the abuser does not see this as a restoration of shalom bayis. Rather, the abuser sees his wife's return as a triumph on his part, and as a capitulation by the wife, by her family, and by the rabbis.* This further inflates his egomania, and his lust for absolute control is increased manifold. It is thus a grave mistake to advise a woman to return to an abusive husband, and those who do so should be aware that they are being accessories and accomplices to the husband's brutality. If the abused wife is subsequently trapped as an *aguna* they must accept a share of the blame!

While there is no assurance that the *aguna* problem can be prevented, there is reason to believe that a husband may be more amenable to give a *get* at an earlier stage, before his wife has become hopelessly dependent on him and before his ability to dominate has gone to his head to an inordinate degree. Thus, if the abuse is recognized when there are no children to the marriage or even one child, the husband's sense of absolute power is much less than when there are seven children. If the abuse is recognized at a stage when the wife is younger and has greater opportunity to become self-sufficient, the husband's sense of power is less than when she is totally dependent on him economically.

Early diagnosis of cancer does not guarantee a cure, but the likelihood of a cure is far greater than when the malignancy has been allowed to take a firm hold. Early diagnosis of abuse and proper evaluation may reveal the marriage to be non-viable, and the attempt to obtain a *get* at this point may be much more successful than years later when the abuser feels himself to be supreme and in total control.

I am not one to treat marriage lightly. I am as much an enthusiast of preserving a marriage and of attaining *shalom bayis* as anyone else, and I will go to great lengths to discourage impulsive breakups of couples who just "don't seem to get along." I am not willing to accept that every claim of incompatibility is valid. I believe that if two adults felt sufficiently attracted to each other to make a commitment to marriage, there may be enough positive factors that may make the relationship viable.

All this notwithstanding, I take a very critical view in cases where there has been abuse, whether it is tyrannical control or battering. I do not automatically recommend dissolving the relationship, but if there has been physical abuse, I insist on prompt separation for the sake of safety, to be followed by a thorough evaluation of what is going on in the marriage, and whether there is a realistic chance of change. In the case of emotional abuse, separation may not be necessary, but adequate evaluation and counseling are absolutely essential. If after all this is done and it appears that there is not enough reason to expect significant change, then the marriage should be terminated rather than permitted to drag on with creation of more difficulties and bringing more children into an unsuccessful relationship, as has been discussed above and in previous chapters.

We must open our eyes to reality and put our minds into high gear. There are few situations among the many varieties of *tzoros* that can compare to the plight of an *aguna*. People who are in a position to minimize such disasters should be well-versed in the problems of wife abuse, to be able to provide proper guidance and counseling. No one should have the plight of an *aguna* on his conscience.

Chapter 24

Child Abuse and Molestation

I assume that by now the reader understands why this book is found in the non-fiction section. The stories are too real. Of course, they could all be fabrications, but let me assure you that I have tried to write fiction and I just do not have the knack for it. The accounts you have read are true.

But whereas the Jewish husband may conceivably be a wife abuser, it is certainly impossible for Jewish parents to be child abusers. Here we have an iron clad tradition that extols the self-sacrifice which Jewish parents will endure for their children's sake. In our prayers we ask G-d to be considerate of us "just as a father has mercy on his children," and who could possibly be more indulgent than "a Yiddishe momma?" The whole idea of any parent abusing a child is abominable, but for Jewish parents to harm a child is simply unthinkable.

We have had to make peace with many unthinkable things. And just as physical child abuse can occur in a Jewish family, we must also unfortunately accept that sexual molestation can occur.

It is tragic for anyone to suffer. We have spent much of this book on the subject of the abused wife, who is so often defenseless. But what could possibly be worse than inflicting harm on a small child, who is totally at the mercy of adults, even to a greater extent than a wife is at the mercy of a tyrannical husband? With all the obstacles and difficulties that an abused wife may encounter, she is nevertheless an adult, and conceivably could take some steps in her own defense. This is not true of a child, who has no avenue of help.

The scars that are left on a child, whether through physical, emotional, or sexual abuse may be permanent. There can be no greater crime than inflicting permanent harm on a young life.

Yet this happens too often. Adults who have children within their power may abuse this power, whether they be parents, teachers, or surrogates, and invariably the abused child bears his pain in silence.

I am not going to elaborate on the all-important subject of the various types of child abuse, because I am not a child psychiatrist or psychologist, and I do not have adequate direct clinical experience to speak intelligently and authoritatively about the subject. I can only try to alert people to the fact that these problems do occur in the Jewish home, and as with wife abuse, there is no immunity. Child abuse and molestation may occur in homes where we would least expect it. I urge child clinicians to provide first hand, comprehensive data on this vital subject, and for everyone in the community to give their utmost attention to this problem and to do whatever it takes to uproot it. Concealing the problem only serves to perpetuate it, and as distasteful as it may be, the community must confront the problem even at the risk of exposure.

The issue of mandatory reporting must be looked at carefully and clarified. There is often reluctance by neighbors, relatives, and teachers to report child abuse. Should one report suspected child abuse or only when one knows for certain? Children do fall and injure themselves, and if an overzealous teacher reports the case of a child who was injured in a fall as one of child abuse, will the family be unfairly harassed? What should be done when one is not certain? How can one investigate in order to discover the truth? It is clear that everything must be done to protect the child from abuse, but by the same token, false reporting may cause harm to the child and the entire family.

This and other issues require a great deal of enlightenment, and there is a need for extensive education and training for parents, educators, counselors, and rabbis. The area of child abuse is a subject for a whole book, and I touched on it only because of the strong correlation between spouse abuse and child abuse.

Children, even tots of four and five need to begin to learn how to protect themselves against molestation, and what and how and whom to tell. In many instances molestation has gone on for years, but children were afraid to report it. There are now books that teach children respect for their own body and that their privacy is sacrosanct, not to be invaded by anyone, including family members, and this is presented in a manner that young children can understand. The whole concept of discipline needs to be reviewed. Clearly children need discipline and sometimes punishment is necessary. How should one use punishment so that it is constructive, and at what point does one cross the line from punishment to abuse?

It has been said that proper living is like walking a tightrope. One must keep a delicate balance, and leaning too far to one side is just as disastrous as leaning too far to the other. To avoid proper discipline is detrimental to the child, who must learn to respect authority and that there are limitations to what he may do. Too much permissiveness does not prepare a child for life in the real world. By the same token, an excess of strictness and punishment that is not commensurate with the child's behavior can be oppressive and crushing to a child's ego.

Parenting is the single greatest responsibility a person has, and this responsibility is shared by educators. The Talmud says that a person who teaches a child carries the same responsibility as a parent (*Sanhedrin* 19B). It is a mistake to assume that every person is born with intuitive parenting skills, and it is equally as wrong to assume that anyone who thinks he can be a teacher is inherently suited for that function.

One may ask, "Parenting and teaching have been going on since time immemorial, and all these generations have survived without formal courses. Why the sudden concern and need for intensive training in these roles?"

My response is that the world also survived before the advent of antibiotics and immunization. Would anyone apply the same logic to avoid these lifesaving techniques? Yes, the world as a whole did survive, but there were many, many casualties which are now avoidable. This is as true of emotional child rearing as of physical child rearing.

Secondly, today's world is not the same world as that of the past. There were always crime and corruption in the world and there was always immorality, but never on the scale that prevails in today's world. The child that was raised in the *shtetl* was not exposed to the toxic environment to which the modern child is exposed. We do need innovative techniques to help us raise and teach children so that they are best prepared to live decent, constructive, and happy lives.

Both young parents and prospective parents could benefit greatly from classes in parenting. In fact, it would be an invaluable contribution to child rearing for classes in parenting to be given to young men and young women in the third and fourth years of high school. After all, these are the parents of the future, and preparation for optimal parenting is certainly far superior to trying to later undo the consequences of parental mistakes.

No one segment of the population can achieve this alone. There must be a common, consistent, and cooperative effort by all those who exert influence on the child in order to provide an optimum result. This includes the nuclear family, the extended family, the school, the clergy, and even the media. While we are not responsible for things that are beyond our control, we do have a sacred responsibility to do everything that is within our means to enable a child to fulfill himself to the full potential with which he was created.

Chapter 25

Counseling and Therapy

We live in an age of specialization. Medical science has advanced rapidly, and there is so much more that is known about every organ system today that there is a real need for specialists, who can focus their attention to the details and nuances of a complicated problem. Yet, the majority of medical problems can be managed satisfactorily by a generalist or family practitioner, who may enlist the services of a specialist when necessary. Doctors who may not have specialized in any one field know enough about the various physical afflictions to either treat them adequately themselves or call upon a specialist when greater expertise is required.

This is often not true in psychology or psychiatry. The denial that prevails among individuals with certain conditions prevails in the educational community as well. As an illustration, it has been demonstrated that thirty percent of all general hospital stays are due to consequences of alcoholism or drug abuse. One might assume that thirty percent of the medical student curriculum would therefore be directed to learning about these conditions. This is not the case. Most medical school curricula do not have twenty-five percent of their time devoted to alcoholism or drug addiction, nor twenty percent nor ten percent nor five percent. . .but, more like .04 percent, or four hours every four-year period. That, incidentally, is four hours more than I received on the subject! After completing medical school I went on to a three-year residency in psychiatry where I again received zero hours of instruction on these vital subjects. Some educational programs have undergone change since the days when I was in school, but some are still grossly derelict in these areas.

The same holds true for various other "social" disorders, i.e., gambling, eating disorders, and yes, spouse abuse. It is possible to become a board certified psychiatrist without having much if any training in problems of domestic violence. As a result, some therapists may not inquire about spouse abuse, and if they do ask and it is denied, they may not realize that the denial has no validity.

When there is a problem which involves one of the conditions that may have been neglected in a therapist's training, one must be careful to consult a therapist who knows something about the problem. Just as there are psychiatrists who know little about alcoholism or drug addiction, there are therapists who know little about domestic violence or emotional spouse abuse.

The best psychiatrist or psychologist in town may not be the right person to consult for a spouse abuse problem. Referral to a competent therapist may be obtained by calling a local shelter or a hotline and asking for names of people who are qualified in this area. There are psychiatrists, psychologists, social workers, and rabbis who have learned the facts of life about these problems and who can do a good evaluation and provide competent counseling.

The therapist for the abused wife should generally be a woman. In a culture where male dominance and male superiority is still a widely held attitude, a victimized woman may not feel she can trust a male therapist. Also, there are issues of intimacy which a woman may find difficult to share with a male therapist. There is also some merit in a woman seeing another woman as a strong person, which may help counteract her feelings of gender-oriented inadequacy.

The abusing husband should see a male therapist, but again, only one who has achieved expertise in management of abuse problems. Therapists who lack such expertise are apt to be taken in by the husband's assigning all blame to the wife. Furthermore, the husband is apt to be in gross denial of his abusive behavior, and an untrained therapist may believe his account as valid.

Abusing husbands are often reluctant to see a therapist, because to them it is demeaning and they may see this as an admission of guilt. They may agree only to see someone together, and in the early phases of treatment, this is generally counterproductive.

Many counselors, therapists, and rabbis, may wish to see the couple in conjoint therapy. After all, the problem is within the relationship, hence is it not logical to address both members of the relationship together?

Conjoint therapy in abuse is actually contraindicated. The woman is usually reluctant to speak of abuse in the presence of her husband for fear of his later retaliation. The discomfort in talking about abuse may cause all three participants, wife, husband, and counselor to avoid the subject and focus on extraneous issues.

Inherent in conjoint therapy is the concept that both partners share equal responsibility for the problem. If abuse is properly understood to be a crime, it becomes obvious that the criminal and his victim do *not* share equal responsibility.

Couples' treatment is typically directed at communication problems and dynamics regarding interaction. It generally does not address the important issues such as what the woman can do to protect herself, or extricate herself if necessary, or psychological issues such as her unwarranted low self-esteem. It generally does not deal with the husband's beliefs regarding male domination, his difficulty in controlling his anger, and his need to be in control of his wife.

It is important that the abusing husband receive therapy, firstly to begin to work on changing his abusive behavior, and secondly, to prevent any self-destruction. Where there has been physical violence, the degree of danger of further beatings necessitates separation and it is not unusual for the batterer to become severely depressed and even suicidal if the wife leaves him. The relationship between a batterer and the wife may be a very bizarre one, where she accepts the abusive behavior because she is totally dependent on him, and he needs her to be dependent on him and to accept his rage. The batterer's reaction to his wife's leaving may therefore be very traumatic.

Group therapy, both for the abused wife and abusive husband is particularly effective. Each one can recognize that they are not alone, and that there are others who understand and empathize with them. Sharing of experiences can be both supportive and therapeutic, as resistances break down and valuable insights are obtained.

It is not unusual for an abused wife to be apprehensive about treatment. She may feel that she must keep this hidden from her husband, because he may become enraged and more abusive if he discovers that she is seeking help. She may elicit the therapist's help in concealment, and set up signals for communicating with her without revealing that she is in therapy. There may be problems in paying for therapy, since the woman may have to concoct stories to explain where the money went. Although in other psychotherapeutic situations the therapist may opt for full honesty and avoid any subterfuges, the nature of this problem necessitates concealment to protect the woman from an irate husband's reaction.

Traditionally, psychotherapy involves searching into the past and discovering the incidents or conflicts that may have been responsible for the development of emotional disorders. The merit of this method has been subject to serious question lately, and more recent psychotherapy is directed to discontinuing the pathological behavior first, and leaving the insights to a later time. In the management of abuse, whether physical or emotional, this is absolutely essential. Abusive behavior must be brought to a screeching halt, and only later can one examine the reason for the abuser's behavior and the wife's tolerance of it.

At this point in time, reliable therapy can be obtained from staff associated with women's shelters or other services for abused women, or from therapists whom they recommend. Hopefully, educational efforts for all providers of human services will increase awareness of abuse problems and expertise in managing them, but for the present, one must turn to therapists who are competent in this field, and whom an abused woman feels she can safely trust.

When there is a physical problem, it is best to begin with a general practitioner, who can refer to a specialist if necessary. In the case of spouse abuse, one must seek out the specialist on one's own.

Chapter 26

Problems Can Occur in Either Direction

While the available statistics indicate that physical abuse in a marriage is committed by the husband against the wife in a ratio of 16:1 as compared to wife against the husband, the incidence of *emotional* abuse where the wife is the abuser is greater than the wife's being *physically* abusive.

Emotional abuse consists of controlling and degrading the spouse, depriving him or her of due respect and dignity. While the aggressive husband may utilize his position as provider or a culturally accepted role as superior to dominate the wife, there are ways in which the wife may exert control.

There is probably no way to state just what comprises a "normal" marriage. There is no one ideal pattern of relationships. It is possible, for example, that there may be a husband who is rather unassertive and does not particularly like to make decisions. The wife may be more assertive, and may set the tone and make most of the decisions in the family, in consultation with the husband. There may be mutual respect, and the atmosphere in the home may be loving and wholesome.

However, if the wife has a need to control and dominate, assertiveness may deteriorate into disregarding the husband's opinion and disparaging him, sometimes belittling him in front of the children. In order to preserve peace in the family, a passive husband may resign himself to this role. His suggestion at marital counseling, if he does make it, may be rejected, and if the wife has a need to control and if she senses his passivity, it is possible that she may become as tyrannical as an abusive husband.

Even if the husband is the sole provider for the family, he may not wish to leave the family because of his love for the wife and children, and his desire to keep the family intact for the children's sake. Culturally, his leaving the marriage might be seen as desertion for which he would be condemned. The wife's parents may threaten to smear him if he leaves the family. Finally, setting up housekeeping for himself while providing adequately for his wife and children may be financially unrealistic. For all these reasons, the husband may be trapped in an abusive relationship.

People who are emotionally healthy do not have the need to dominate and belittle others. Men and women who have such needs are sick people, and while they can be helped, they would have to recognize a need for help. Most often people who are emotionally abusive are self-righteous and place all blame on others, hence they see no reason whatsoever why they should seek counseling. These unhappy relationships may thus continue indefinitely.

The only thing that may bring such a couple into counseling is a crisis, usually something involving one of the children. I have seen a number of cases where an adolescent was admitted for treatment of a drug or alcohol problem, and in the process of treating the whole family, the abusive character of the parental relationship became evident. With good counseling, both parents came to realize that the relationship was detrimental to both themselves and the children, and were able to make constructive changes in the marriage.

Parents have a great investment in their children, and when they realize that an abusive relationship exerts a deleterious effect on their children, they may be motivated to examine their relationship and improve its quality. It is unfortunate that such insight may come only at the cost of crisis with one or more of their children, but it is not unusual for pathological lifestyles to continue until they are interrupted by some "rock bottom" trauma.

Many husbands and wives may love each other deeply, and when emotional abuse occurs in either direction, they may feel helpless to do anything about it. If it is addressed at an early stage and proper counseling is sought, much harm can be averted, and the relationship can flourish. At this stage there may be no need for any major upheavals. If the emotional abuse is allowed to continue, it may become more intense and more encompassing, and result in frustration and anger which may impact upon and diminish the love. This is detrimental to everyone concerned: husband, wife, children, and even the extended family.

I therefore appeal to husbands and wives to be aware that we are all capable of acting abusively to those whom we love, *without being aware that we are doing so,* and if this were pointed out to us, we would eliminate behavior which is not becoming to us. Therefore, if your spouse complains about how you are acting toward him or her, do not react defensively. Sometimes the problem can be identified and eliminated with just a bit better communication between the couple. If necessary, help of a competent counselor should be enlisted to ease the communication problems and eliminate obstacles to a healthy relationship. Seeking competent counseling is not an insult, not an accusation, and not an admission of defeat. It is the sensible thing to do, to preserve the most sacred of human relationships, and to provide a wholesome environment for children.

Chapter 27

A Good Beginning

While denial still prevails over much of the Jewish community, the past decade has shown some signs of stirring. Much more needs to be done, but there is now at least a nucleus of hope.

Many communities have at least given some recognition to the existence of the problem of wife abuse by organizing lectures and panels. Anglo-Jewish periodicals have carried articles on the subject. Some federations and foundations are organizing and supporting courses to educate service providers in the Jewish community about the problem of abuse. Some rabbinical organizations are holding workshops on the subject. A number of communities have hotlines, and in some of the larger Jewish communities there are established shelters. Unfortunately, in some communities the Jewish Family Services, while interested in the problem and recognizing its seriousness, do not have adequate staff to deal with it, and some say that they have a "waiting list." This makes about as much sense as having a waiting list at the fire department or rescue squad. Wife abuse is an emergency problem, which requires prompt response and immediate access to help.

The following are the resources known to me at the time of publication, and I apologize for any omissions:

CHICAGO, IL
SHALVAH
24 hour hotline for Jewish women
Counseling, legal aid, community education
(312) 583-4673

CLEVELAND, OH
PROJECT CHAI
Jewish Family Services
24 hour hotline, emergency housing, financial aid, counseling, vocational training, community education
(216) 292-3999

DETROIT, MI
Jewish Family Services
"Windows"-counseling, safe house, prevention of abuse and neglect
(810) 559-1500

HOUSTON, TX
ADVA
Counseling, legal assistance
(713) 664-2832

Jewish Families Service
Counseling, financial aid, legal aid
(713) 667-9336

LOS ANGELES, CA
EZRAS BAYIS WARMLINE
Orthodox Counseling Program
Jewish Families Service
24 Hour Domestic Violence warmline
(213) 896-0981

MINNEAPOLIS
Jewish Family and Children Services
Counseling, emergency financial aid, family life education programs
(614) 546-0616

MONTREAL, QUEBEC, CANADA
Auberge Pour Femmes
Shelter, counseling, 24 hour support line, support group
(514) 731-0833

NEW CITY, NY
PROJECT TIKVAH
Rockland Family Shelter
Shelter, group and individual counseling
(914) 634-3344

NEW YORK METROPOLITAN AREA
SHALOM TASK FORCE
Referral for shelter and counseling, community education, halachic
consultations
(718) 337-3700

JEWISH BOARD OF FAMILY AND CHILDREN'S
SERVICES, FAR ROCKAWAY
Shelter, counseling, groups for survivors
(718) 520-8045

PHILADELPHIA, PA
Jewish Family and Children's Services
Counseling, support groups
(215) 545-3290

PITTSBURGH, PA
Jewish Family and Children's Services
Family counseling, support groups, court accompaniment, referral to
shelters, medical and legal aid
(412) 256-4900

TORONTO, ONTARIO, CANADA
Jewish Families and Children's Services
Safe House, counseling, financial aid, support group
(416) 638-7800

**In communities other than those above, contact your local Jewish
Families Services.**

While this is a good beginning, it is still only a beginning. Our
awareness of the scope of the problem may be the tip of the iceberg,
and the needs for service may correspond to the immensity of the
entire iceberg.

Even in communities where shelters exist, there may not be adequate services and funding to provide the necessary comprehensive assistance for the abused wife and her children, as was outlined in an earlier chapter. More of everything is required, much more.

My fondest dream is that in the years ahead the list of resources for abused wives would actually be smaller as a result of significant substantive advances in preventing this tragic problem. But dreams are just that, fantasy rather than reality. Until the millennium materializes, we must have more communities coming forth with efforts of greater empathy, greater understanding, greater involvement at all levels of service providers, and greater access to facilities for help.

BIBLIOGRAPHY

Schechter, Susan and Ann Jones, *When Love Goes Wrong - What to Do When You Can't Do Anything Right: Strategies for Women with Controlling Partners.* New York: Harper Collins, 1992

McDermott, Judith and Frances Wells Burck, *Children of Domestic Violence: Healing the Wounds.* A Guide for Moms: A Project of Rockland Family Shelter, 1990.

NiCarthy, Ginny, *Getting Free: A Handbook For Women in Abusive Relationships.* Seattle: The Seal Press, 1982